Pre-K Teacher's Gu

Get Set for School™ Pre–K Workbook

Get Set for School™ Sing Along CD

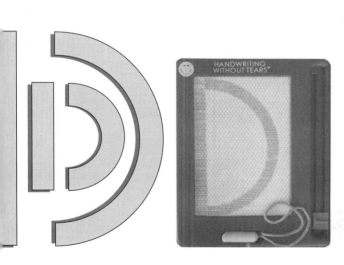

Wood Pieces Set Stamp and See Screen™

Roll–A–Dough Letters™

Mat Man™

by Jan Z. Olsen, OTR
Developer of the Handwriting Without Tears® Curriculum

Handwriting Without Tears®
Jan Z. Olsen, OTR

8001 MacArthur Blvd
Cabin John, MD 20818
Phone: 301–263–2700 • Fax: 301–263–2707
www.hwtears.com • JanOlsen@hwtears.com

Foreword

Hello, I'm Emily Knapton, I'm an occupational therapist and a colleague of Jan Olsen's. Below is a picture of my daughter Abigail. After taking the Handwriting Without Tears® (HWT) workshop in 1998, I began using the strategies with my students in the public schools. My success using HWT made me want to share it with others. Eventually, I joined Jan at HWT, and as an HWT workshop presenter I now train teachers, therapists and parents across the country. At every course, I had questions about what's appropriate for preschoolers. Many requests led HWT to believe that we must do something for preschoolers.

Jan Olsen asked for my help with the preschool program; Get Set for School™. Often she was asking not just for my help but for Abi's help. Abi is an in-house expert on what works with preschoolers. Not only did she willingly try out the songs, the activities and the workbook pages, she has posed for many of the illustrations in this guide.

What passed the "Abi Test" was deemed worthy of being tried on other preschoolers. Jan and I have tried out the workbook pages, songs, and activities with children in the Omaha, NE and Washington, DC area. We don't believe in pushing academics or teaching regular kindergarten work to preschool children. Instead, HWT wanted a developmentally appropriate, positive program that would work for this age group. It has been a joy to see children respond so positively to the program. The HWT Pre-K program is exciting and fun. It will help your students Get Set For School™.

Introduction

Welcome to our Pre–K program, Get Set for School™. I'm Jan Olsen, an occupational therapist and the developer of the Handwriting Without Tears® curriculum. When my own son was crying about printing in the first grade, I used task analysis and my OT background to create a simple, developmentally based way to teach children handwriting. Today, millions of children benefit from being taught Handwriting Without Tears.® Look at our website www.hwtears.com to learn more about the curriculum.

Now we have a Pre–K program to meet the needs of younger children. The Pre–K year is a year of preparation. But giving little children the same work they'll get in kindergarten is not good. They simply aren't ready and there are other, more important things for them to be doing. This program is designed to prepare them but to do it in a playful way that is child–friendly and developmentally sound.

Happily, Pre–K teachers are very sensitive to developmental differences, the early and late bloomers, younger and older children. This *Pre–K Teacher's Guide* follows a developmental sequence. This makes it easy for teachers to decide what activities to use and when to introduce new activities.

This program will fit right in with what good, developmentally based teachers have always believed and done. But we have exciting new materials and ways to help children develop readiness skills for kindergarten. We wanted music to be an important part of the program. We wanted fun! When you listen to the CD, you'll hear not just Cathy and Marcy, who are fabulous, but also children. In the recording studio, they were begging to sing extra parts. We think your children will love the music too.

As we tested new activities like Mat Man™, we taped the children and reviewed their before and after drawings. We found ourselves saying. "Look at this. The improvement is just amazing." Then as we reviewed the videos over and over, we realized that something even more important was happening. The children were so happy, relaxed and eager as they participated. We loved the giggling.

Jan Z. Olsen

Learning Magazine
**2005 Winner
Teacher's Choice Award**

Association for
Educational Publishers
**2004 Winner
Children's Curriculum**

With profound gratitude, I thank:

Emily Knapton, OTR/L, a bright and gifted therapist. Since joining HWT, she has been an energetic and enthusiastic colleague. She is passionate about preschoolers and the quality of the program reflects her many contributions. It has been a joy to work with Emily.

Leah Connor, a webpage and graphic designer par excellence. She has cranked out page after page, design after design, book after book, with unfailing good humor, talent, and speed. Leah amazes us all.

© 2005 Jan Z. Olsen

Building a Foundation

Helping children develop a strong foundation is very important work and you are important! As you teach Pre–K students, you'll enjoy them because younger children are fun, but you'll especially enjoy watching them as they blossom in the learning environment you create. Children are so active and eager to try new things. But, because ability levels vary greatly at this age, it is essential to meet children exactly where they are developmentally. Start by focusing on their strengths and their interests. Then, when you think they're ready, gradually move them to develop new abilities in areas that are more challenging.

The Handwriting Without Tears® Get Set for School™ curriculum is designed to encompass foundation skills for successful learning. How well children succeed in school and life depends on the people in their lives and their early environment. The HWT Pre–K program is designed to help you create an optimal learning experience in the following areas:

Playing and Singing: Children love to play. It's how they learn. By playing with one another, children not only learn valuable concepts, they learn how to socialize and get along with others. That's why so many of the activities for younger children are play based. They play with Wood Pieces, Mat Man™ and Roll–A–Dough Letters™. Children love music. Parents and teachers who sing to their children impart a basic love for music and tap into the very rhythm of life. There is so much joy and learning when children move, sing, and tap to music. HWT believes this is such an important part of child development that we've created a special Sing Along CD with Cathy Fink and Marcy Marxer. These two musicians are award winning musicians, renown for their work with children.

Motor: Movement uses big muscles (gross motor) and small muscles (fine motor). Motor skills enable children to explore, participate and interact in their environment. Motor skills are important for school success on the playground and in the classroom. Children need to develop strength and stamina. The HWT Pre–K program and Sing Along CD have activities and songs that encourage children to move and use their muscles. Many of these activities involve imitating the teacher's motions. The ability to imitate the teacher and to respond to the teacher through movement is one of the most important foundation skills for school success.

Social/Emotional: Children who feel safe and successful in their environment naturally enjoy participating and being involved with others. The HWT Pre–K program has something for every child. Almost every lesson or activity is designed so that all children can participate but they may be participating at different developmental levels. For example, the wood piece activity is one in which a group of children sit together on the floor and rub the four basic wood piece shapes. Children may be learning the size and shape words for the four different wood pieces...or figure ground visual discrimination...or just to sit with the group...or to talk to a classmate...or manipulative skills. But each child is developing a sense of belonging and an eagerness to participate and learn.

Cognitive/Language: The activities in the HWT Pre–K program use a child friendly, structured approach to tasks and language. The activities are designed to methodically and consistently teach the words children need to follow directions. When children really know the meaning of words such as top/middle/bottom, big/little, line/curve, my turn/your turn, under/over, start/stop, they can easily understand and follow directions. They can participate and complete tasks with confidence.

Sensory: Our senses help us learn and give us pleasure and information. The multi–sensory activities in this program are planned to appeal to all learning styles and preferences. Some children are primarily visual learners, others learn best by listening. Some like to be moving and touching everything and some want to avoid getting messy. All children can benefit from using their favorite and familiar learning style and from trying out new sensational ways to learn. Often just seeing their friends enjoy and participate helps children expand their acceptance of sensory experiences. Multi–sensory activities alleviate boredom, enhance attention and make learning more fun.

Visual Perceptual: Pre–K is a year of preparation for kindergarten. Until now, children have been learning in the three dimensional, real world. Next year, the focus of much of their learning will be on symbols—letters and numbers. We want to keep children playing, manipulating and learning in an active three–dimensional world. But, we can use activities that will sharpen their visual skills, teach them basic habits, and get them oriented and organized for symbols. Children can learn basic habits for shapes and sizes, letters and numbers. They become oriented to how the English language works; that reading and writing go from top to bottom, left to right. If they start to write a few letters and numbers, they'll use good habits that will serve them well next year.

Table of Contents

Take a Look at Pre-K

Pre-Kindergarten Teacher's Guide

- Guide for the Pre–K workbook *Get Set for School™*
- Readiness activities for children of all ability levels
- Lesson plans for developing body awareness, good habits, coloring, drawing and handwriting skills
- Tips for using: Wood Pieces, *Get Set for School™ Sing Along* CD, Stamp and See Screen, and Roll–A–Dough Letters™

Get Set for School™ Sing Along CD

When 2004 and 2005 Grammy Award Winning Artists, Cathy Fink and Marcy Marxer bring their talents to Handwriting Without Tears® the curriculum sings, taps, and dances! Learning the ABC's is so much fun when a dog comes to school and has to sing the ABC's. Numbers are easy when children sing about counting legs. For 6, it's "The Ant, The Bug, and The Bee" song. The songs and finger–plays on the *Get Set for School™ Sing Along* CD will delight and teach your children.
See Pages 84–93

Capital Letter Wood Pieces Set

The Capital Letter Wood Pieces set includes 26 pieces: 8 big lines, 6 little lines, 6 big curves, and 6 little curves. Use wood pieces to teach basic size, shape and position concepts. Wood pieces help children develop their fine motor, vocabulary and figure ground discrimination skills. By choosing pieces and placing them correctly, children learn to form capital letters.
See Pages 6–14, 24–26

Roll–A–Dough Letters™

Here's a product that meshes all the fun of dough and the advantages of the HWT curriculum. Use the tray with letter and number cards to delight and teach at the same time. The tray may also be used to make letters in sand or shaving cream. Set includes a plastic 4" x 6" tray, laminated letter and number cards and 12 oz of dough.
See Page 27

Slate Chalkboard

The chalkboard is made of real slate, measuring 4" x 6", in a sturdy wood frame. The ☺ at the top left corner orients children and reinforces top to bottom, left to right directionality.
See Pages 29–30, 77

Get Set for School™ Pre-K Workbook

Get Set for School™ is a "crayon only" workbook for four year olds or older students at a Pre–K level. The workbook begins with coloring pages to develop color and shape recognition. This easy–to–do workbook uses a developmental sequence for shapes, pre–strokes, letters and numbers.
See Pages 39–83

Capital Letter Wood Pieces and Mat

Build Mat Man™ and sing the "Mat Man™" song! This floor activity develops body awareness, position concepts, and pre–drawing skill. Mat Man™ is a real class pleaser for encouraging social participation and taking turns. Also use Wood Pieces to develop stopping/starting, listening, singing and position skills. When children are ready, teach letters and numbers with the wood pieces and mat.
See Pages 18–21, 26

Capital Letter Cards for Wood Pieces

The Capital Letter Cards are ideal for children who are just learning capital letters. The set includes 26 double–sided cards. The front of each card shows a single capital letter made with wood pieces and is used to teach children the stroke sequence for forming the capital letter. The back of each card has four beginning activities to help teach letter awareness.
See Pages 24–25

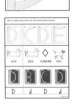

Stamp and See Screen™

Stamp and See Screen™ is a magnetic screen that measures 4" x 6" in a sturdy plastic frame. The 4 wooden magnetic pieces (big line, little line, big curve, little curve) allow children to stamp capital letters. A tool resembling chalk can be used to trace or write capital letters. The slide eraser clears the board so it can be used over and over.
See Page 28

The Pre-K Environment

Outside Play

Outside play develops upper and lower body strength and stability. In addition to the health benefits of outdoor exercise, there are social and cognitive benefits as well. Safety rules and routines for taking turns help children learn to play cooperatively. Spatial awareness and language skills grow as children move and hear the teacher say, "You are **up** at the **top** now. It's time to come **down** now so we can go **inside.**" Riding toys and construction toys help children with their sense of directionality, weight, force and balance. The freedom to change activities, to be active or quiet, social or alone is important for emotional balance and well being.

Music

Music is always important, but especially so at this age. There's music to soothe the resting child. Then there's music to get up and move about, dance and shout! With repetitive lyrics children learn words and concepts effortlessly. For some children, it is music that unlocks language skills. Play the *Get Set For School*™ Sing Along CD for your children and incorporate the songs and activities in your daily activities. The songs and fingerplays are designed to encourage children to listen, move and imitate.

Messy Play

Preschool teachers are so wise. They recognize the importance of direct sensory experience in learning. We added Roll–A–Dough Letters™ to the sensory repertoire. This product has a tray, dough and letter cards. Children practice making letters in many ways using different materials including dough, sand, shaving cream, and lotion. It's a sensory activity that develops letter skills. Some children don't like messy play or react negatively to touch. If gentle, gradual approaches don't work, ask an occupational therapist or pediatrician for advice.

Pretending and Building

Sturdy timeless toys (wood blocks, dress up clothes, kitchens, farm animals, people, cars etc.) invite children to a world of imagination and self-directed play. In play like this, children are active in moving, turning, and placing objects. The Pre–K curriculum expands block play to include play with flat wood pieces. Four basic shapes (big lines/little lines, big curves/little curves) are rubbed, sorted, stacked and positioned to make shapes and letters.

Drawing and Painting

Drawing is the trace of movement! Encourage children to discover the relationship between how they move and the marks they make with finger paint, sand and shaving cream. Children learn by exploration but it's fine to sometimes show them how to move the fingers and hand to create dots, wiggles, lines and circles. Just dropping the arm down makes lines. So does pulling across. Swinging the arm around makes circles. Give children small broken pieces of crayon for drawing. The little pieces promote the use and strength of the fingertips for holding. Later, this will facilitate the use of the correct tripod grip for holding the pencil.

Circle Time, Stories and Fingerplays

Picture books and stories are staples. Add hand motions, fingerplays and responses to circle activities to increase participation and attention. Discover new group and circle activities throughout this guide.

The Pre-K Environment, cont.

Easel Art

Children can work and move freely when they stand before an easel. Standing up and working against gravity helps build strength in the shoulders and arms. This surface is ideal for wrist position too. It is quite natural for children to hold the wrist in a comfortable, neutral position at the easel. Try turning an old bi-fold door into a big community easel. Children who are less experienced will learn by imitating others. Because it's a communal picture, there is no concern about the final product. It's as appealing as graffiti. Encourage children to move places freely, to come and go as they please. Put small baskets of colored chalk and crayon on the table.

Table Activities

Use a variety of table and chair sizes. Children come in different sizes and so should furniture. It is important to have the right height for coloring and working on puzzles etc. Try to avoid putting children directly across from each other. When children work face to face, they may copy the other child's work upside down and backwards. Putting something in the middle of the table will help prevent this problem.

Turn the tables so that the children face you when you're demonstrating or drawing for them. You want them to clearly see your arm and hand as you draw. This builds important associations between movement and lines. Draw simple shapes for children and turn them into animals or pictures. Another reason for children to be facing you is that they can hear you more clearly when they're looking directly at you.

Pre-Writing Center

Turn a table area into a pre-writing center. Children love to make cards, letters or pretend grocery lists. Stickers, stamps, labels and envelopes add to the fun. Tape, scissors, glue and catalogs are appealing and useful in developing fine motor skills. Do not be concerned about "play writing." We never want children to develop bad habits by making children write before they're ready or telling them to write. But self initiated, spontaneous, play writing is fine.

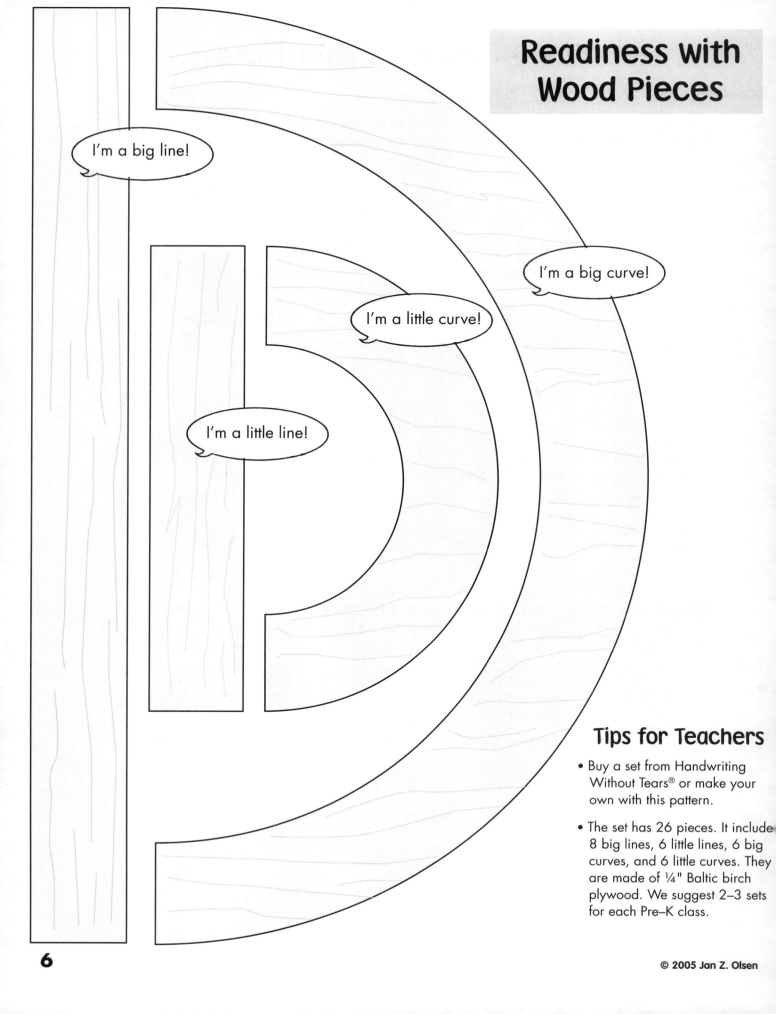

Readiness with Wood Pieces

I'm a big line!

I'm a big curve!

I'm a little curve!

I'm a little line!

Tips for Teachers

- Buy a set from Handwriting Without Tears® or make your own with this pattern.

- The set has 26 pieces. It include 8 big lines, 6 little lines, 6 big curves, and 6 little curves. They are made of ¼" Baltic birch plywood. We suggest 2–3 sets for each Pre–K class.

6

Wood Pieces on the Floor

Polish Wood Pieces Together

Working with the Wood Pieces Set is a fun and relaxed way to teach children the concepts of and the words to describe size and shape. This activity prepares children for making capital letters.

Show children how to polish, stack, and sort the wood pieces. This is a friendly, relaxed, and worthwhile activity that children love. Talk about the pieces. Gradually, the children will pick up the important words (big line, little line, big curve, little curve) along with the pieces!

"You have a big curve. I have a big curve. We picked the same pieces."
"You have a big line. I have a big curve. Do you want to trade?"
"Let's polish lines. Do you want to polish a big line or a little line?"
"It's time to collect the wood pieces. Who has a big line?"

Wood Pieces on the Floor Help Children

- **Size and Shape**—Children can feel and see the difference between big and little, line and curve.
- **Vocabulary**—Children begin to use consistent words (big line, little line, big curve, little curve) to describe the wood pieces.
- **Social Skills**—Children learn to work together, share, trade, pay attention, and imitate.
- **Bi-lateral Hand Skills**—Using one hand to hold a piece while the other rubs helps develop a child's fine motor skills.
- **Visual Skills**—Children begin to see the differences in size and shapes.
- **Figure Ground Discrimination**—Children learn to find a particular piece in an assortment of scattered pieces.

Wood Pieces in the Bag

Find Wood Pieces in a Bag

Children learn with a sense of touch. Prepare for this activity by filling a bag with assorted Capital Letter Wood Pieces. Hold the bag. Child reaches inside, feels one piece, guesses which piece it is, and then takes it out.

Wood Pieces in the Bag Help Children Develop

- **Tactile Discrimination of Size and Shape**—Children feel the characteristics of the piece they are touching.
- **Vocabulary**—Children use consistent words to describe size and shape (big line, little line, big curve, and little curve).
- **Fine Motor Skills**—Reaching in the bag and manipulating the piece with one hand develops manipulative skills.
- **Taking Turns**—Children learn to wait for their turn.

Tips for Teachers

- You can easily grade this activity just by what you put in the bag. For very young children or children with special needs, put in just two different shapes.
- Make it extra fun by adding objects too, like a ping-pong ball or a spoon. Children will use words that describe the size and shape of these objects.

Hokey Pokey

Do the Hokey Pokey and you turn yourself around
That's what it's all about

You make the big line walk
You make the big line talk—hello hello
You make the big line walk
Then you move it up and down
You do the Hokey Pokey—put the big line down
That's what it's all about

You put the little line in front
You put the little line in back
You put the little line in front
And then you give a little tap—tap tap
You do the Hokey Pokey—put the little line down
That's what it's all about

You put the big curve up
You put the big curve down
You put the big curve up
And you turn yourself around
You do the Hokey Pokey—put the big curve down
That's what it's all about

You make the little curve wait
You make the little curve skate
You make the little curve wait
And then you skate it all around
You do the Hokey Pokey—put the little curve down
That's what it's all about

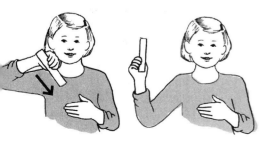

You put the little line in
You take the little line out
You put the little line in
And then you give a little shout—yippee!
You do the Hokey Pokey—put the little line down
That's what it's all about

Wood Pieces Everywhere

Position words like front and back, over and under, and up and down are an important part of a child's language development. These words answer the question, "Where?" Wood Pieces are great for teaching positions in space. Children enjoy watching and imitating what you do and say. This activity helps children understand and follow directions. Some are learning to pay attention, participate, and follow the teacher. Others are learning important language concepts and position words through movement. Everyone develops movement and coordination skills.

TOP
MIDDLE
BOTTOM

Top, middle, bottom are essential words for school. Think of teaching E! Only if children understand "top, middle, bottom" will they be able to follow the teacher's directions.

VERTICAL—STAND UP
HORIZONTAL—LIE DOWN

The actual words, vertical and horizontal, aren't important but the positions are! For fun, pretend that the horizontal line is a sleeping baby. Gently rock the baby, singing "Horizontal... sleeping baby." Then make the baby wake up and stand.

OVER
UNDER

Demonstrate moving the big line over your head or over your arm. Then move it under your arm, under your chin, or under your chair. Talk about sleeping under the covers, or finding lost shoes under the bed. In preschool, there should be lots of real crawling under and over things.

Wood Pieces Everywhere, cont.

FRONT
BACK

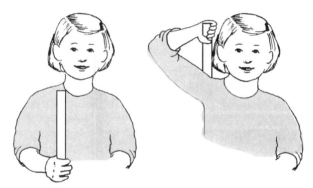

At first just say "front" or "back" with the motions. Tell the children that each child has a front and a back. Use the word "behind." Have them touch their backs with a wood piece and say, "The wood piece is behind me."

IN
OUT

Place one hand across your chest for a pocket. Put the wood piece in the pocket and take it out. Learning the in/out concept begins with early dumping and filling. Dumping is easy, but putting things away or in a container will be a continuing lesson. Talk about inside and outside, too.

UP
DOWN

Put the big line up in the air. Move it down to touch the ground. Look up. "What's up in the sky? Planes, clouds, and birds." Look down. "What falls down? Snow, leaves, and rain!"

APART
TOGETHER

Make sure you have lots of room for this! Use big lines now, but try big curves soon. Do this with just fingers. Spread fingers far apart. Touch fingertips together. You can teach the word BETWEEN by pointing to the place between fingers.

Curves and Circles

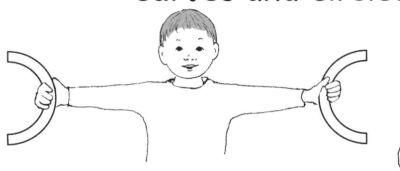 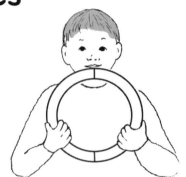

Stand far apart for this one! Say the words, "apart/together" and move those wood pieces! Use big or little curves. Show children how to twirl circles with a soft ball on a string. Make circles by just rotating the arm at an easel too.

O	is a **LETTER.**	Say "O." The mouth makes an O too.
ZERO	is a **NUMBER.**	Show an empty plate. Ask, "How many crackers? Zero."
CIRCLE	is a **SHAPE.**	Draw circles. Start with a C.

HAPPY
SAD

Hold a big curve up. You're happy. Turn it over. You're sad.

RAINBOW

Sing "Somewhere Over the Rainbow." Hold the big curve with one hand and make big curve motions over the rainbow. This helps children associate movements with shape.

Diagonals

Diagonal letters, triangles, and diamonds are developmentally difficult. Wood pieces can make diagonals easy and fun! The actual words "vertical" and "diagonal" are not important. What's important is making diagonals by watching and imitating.

VERTICAL—HELICOPTER
DIAGONAL—JET

Make a big line go up like a helicopter. Now make it take off like a jet.

APART
TOGETHER—AT THE TOP

Start with one big line in each hand, APART and VERTICAL. Now wiggle the tops TOGETHER. This looks like the start of letter A. It needs a little line to be an A.

TOGETHER—AT THE BOTTOM
OPEN—AT THE TOP

Hold two big lines together at the bottom. Say "Abracadabra" and open the top. It's a V. Say, "V for Voila," and say that Voila is the French word for "Here it is!"

For even more fun, help children make their Vs touch to make a W. Use one hand to hold the Vs together at the top.

Diagonals, cont.

**APART
TOGETHER AT THE MIDDLE
TAPPING AT THE MIDDLE**

Start with one big line in each hand, APART and VERTICAL. Now put them together at the middle. It's an X. X marks the spot. Find X on an EXIT sign.

As soon as children put big lines together, they'll start tapping. Tap randomly with them and then make a big show of holding the big lines out and up for silence. Then tap again. Then move them apart for silence.

Now use tapping to teach listening and waiting. It's a "My turn—your turn" game. Children must freeze and not move until the teacher says "Your turn." To start, the teacher says "My turn" and taps twice. The teacher pauses and says, "Your turn." The children tap. Keep the tapping pattern simple until they catch on. Then you can vary the pause, the taps, or the rhythm.

This activity can also be done with the *Get Set for School™ Sing Along* CD, track #19.

Tap, Tap, Tap

Tap, Tap, Tap—Use two big lines to tap, follow rhythm and teacher's motions

Tap, tap, tap big lines, Tap big lines together. Repeat 1X
Tap a little louder now, Tap along with me.
Tap a little softer now, Tap along with me.

Tap, tap, tap big lines, Tap them on the floor Repeat 1X
Play your big lines like a drum, Play along with me
Play your big lines like a drum, Play along with me

Touch, touch, touch big lines, Touch them to your toes
Touch, touch, touch big lines, Touch them to your nose
Touch them on your shoulders now, Don't forget your head
Touch them right down to your knees and everybody sneeze…ACHOO!

Move, move, move big lines, Move them in the air
Move, move, move big lines, Move them under your chair
Move your big lines to the front, Move them to the back
Move your big lines to the side, Now put them in your lap

Tap, tap, tap big lines, Tap them at the top
Tap, tap, tap big lines, Tap 'til I say STOP
11 taps, STOP; Repeat 3X
Now let's try it faster!
11 taps, STOP; Repeat 3X

Suggested Activity
• You can adapt the song by using hands instead of big lines and changing the words in the song.

Body Awareness

Shake Hands with Me

With this amazing activity children learn right/left discrimination and social skills

Gather Materials

Each day choose a different sensory modality. Here are a few suggestions:
Lotion, Water in a bowl, Rubber stamp, Flavoring

Directions

1. Shake hands with each child. Smile, make eye contact, and say "Hello."
2. Immediately say, "This hand is your right hand. I'm going to do something to your right hand."
   Lotion—Put a dab on the right thumb and index finger. "Rub them together."
   Water—Dip right fingers in bowl. "Shake the water off."
   Rubber stamp—Stamp the right hand. "Look at your right hand now."
   Flavoring—Dab some on the right index finger. "Smell that peppermint."
3. Then have the children raise their right hands and say with you:
   - This is my right hand.
   - I shake hands with my right hand.

Shake Hands with Me Helps Children Develop

- **Social Skills**—For meeting and greeting
- **Right/Left Discrimination**—Only the right hand is for shaking
- **Directionality**—A sense of directionality on our own bodies

Shake Hands with a Friend

Another way to teach left and right discrimination is to have children shake hands with a friend. This activity is a wonderful way to encourage socialization and acceptance in the classroom. Try the following activity:

1. Use the *Get Set for School™ Sing Along* CD, choose track #7.
2. Have children stand in pairs.
3. Play the CD. Begin by just singing. Then shake hands and say "Hi" to each other.
4. Have the children shake hands while singing the song.

Hello Song

Little kids can wave bye, bye
But only big kids know
How to stand perfectly still
And say, "Hello"

Give 'em your right hand
Look 'em in the eye
Put a smile on your face
Then you say, "Hi"
Repeat 1X

"It's nice to meet you
How do you do?"
They'll be so happy
To be meeting you
Greetings are a way to say
"I hope you have a wonderful day"

Give 'em your right hand
Look 'em in the eye
Put a smile on your face
Then you say, "Hi"
Repeat 1X

I'm a big kid and I know
To use my right hand when I say hello
To put my right hand for you to take
We meet each other and we shake
Shake, shake, So

Give 'em your right hand
Look 'em in the eye
Put a smile on your face
Then you say, "Hi"
Repeat 3X

Count on Me

Move, Point, and Say Body Parts Together

Children learn body parts by pointing to and naming each body part. This activity also encourages learning the number concepts "1" and "2." We are symmetrically made and our "two" body parts are on our two sides. The "one" body parts are down the center of the body. Fingers and toes are in units of five.

Gather Materials

2 big lines
CD player
Get Set for School™ Sing Along CD

Directions

1. Children stand.
2. Teacher hands out 2 big lines to each student.
3. Teacher begins the chant "Count on Me," track #9.*
4. Teacher demonstrates movements and points to body parts.
5. Children imitate.

*Note: It is recommended that teacher listen to CD to learn the chant and then do the activity with the students without the CD.

Count on Me
Tune: No Tune

You count with me
I'll count with you
I have two big lines
Let's count 1, 2

I have
2 eyebrows
2 eyes
2 ears
2 cheeks
2 lips to smack together

2 shoulders
2 elbows
2 arms
2 wrists
2 hands to clap together

2 hips
2 legs
2 knees
2 ankles
2 feet to tap together

Now that was fun
2 's all done

Now let's do the # 1
1 head
1 forehead
1 nose
1 mouth
1 chin
1 neck
1 chest

Now here's the part I like the best
1 belly button in the middle of me
1 belly button that you can't see

Now let's count fingers
Let's count toes

Fingers
1 2 3 4 5 6 7 8 9 10
10 fingers

Toes
1 2 3 4 5 6 7 8 9 10
10 toes

I'll stop counting right there
I'm not counting teeth or hair

Count on Me Helps Children Develop

- **Body Awareness**—Body parts
- **Number Concepts**—Counting
- **Socialization**—Participation, following directions
- **Motor**—Large motor movements

Suggested Activity

- Fold a paper vertically and cut out a paper doll. The "one" parts are on the fold and the "two" parts are there when you unfold the doll.

Wiggle Your Toes

Toe Song

This fun song teaches the concept of the number 10 by having children play with their own feet while sitting on the floor in a circle. The activity encourages children to take off their own shoes and socks while singing the song with their teacher. Allow extra time for this activity. When it's over, help children put their shoes on and practice shoe tying.

Gather Materials

CD player
Get Set for School™ Sing Along CD

Directions

1. Children sit on the floor in a circle.
2. Teacher plays the CD or begins singing the "Toe Song," track #11.
3. Teacher demonstrates movements to the song (pointing to shoes, taking off shoes, wiggling toes).
4. Children imitate.

Toe Song

You can't see them
But everybody knows
In my shoes, I have 10 toes
5 toes here and 5 toes there
Toes are hiding everywhere

Toes in socks and toes in shoes
Wiggle, wiggle, tippy, tippy toes

At the beach
10 toes come out
They're so happy
They could shout
5 toes here and 5 toes there
Toes are playing everywhere

No more socks and no more shoes
Wiggle, wiggle, tippy, tippy toes
Wiggle, wiggle, tippy, tippy toes
Wiggle, wiggle, tippy, tippy toes

Toe Song Helps Children Develop

- **Body Awareness**—Body parts
- **Number Concepts**—Counting toes
- **Socialization**—Participation, following directions

Suggested Activity

- Mix up children's shoes and sort them.

Mat Man™

Build, Sing, and Draw Mat Man™ Together!

Young children are often asked to draw pictures of themselves or a person. Mat Man™ will make it easy. These activities are social and develop a child's body awareness, drawing and counting skills.

Gather Materials

HWT Mat

Wood Pieces:
- 2 big curves (head)
- 3 little curves (ears, mouth)
- 4 big lines (arms, legs)
- 2 little lines (feet)

Accessories:
- 2 hands
- 2 eyes (small water bottle caps)
- 1 nose (larger milk or juice cap)
- other items as desired

Directions for Building and Singing

1. Children sit on floor in a circle.
2. Teacher quickly builds Mat Man on the floor.
3. Teacher gives Mat Man's parts away.
4. Children build Mat Man as they sing the "Mat Man" song with the teacher.
5. Extra accessories will make Mat Man more interesting or into a different Mat Person (belly button, hair, clothing, seasonal items).

Directions for Drawing

1. Children sit at tables/desks facing teacher.
   Teacher draws a large Mat Man at the board or easel.
2. Teacher draws each part in order.
   Sing/say: "Mat Man has one head. Watch me draw the head. Now it's your turn!"
3. Encourage children to add other details to their drawings.

Mat Man™ Helps Children Develop

- **Body Awareness**—Body parts, body functions
- **Drawing Skills**—Placing body parts correctly, sequencing and organization
- **Socialization**—Participation, following directions, contributing taking turns
- **Number Awareness**—Counting body parts

Mat Man™

Show children how to build Mat Man™ using the HWT Mat, Capital Letter Wood Pieces and a few accessories.

Mat Man™

Tune: *The Bear Went Over the Mountain*

Mat Man has	1 head,	1 head,	1 head,	Mat Man has	1 head,	So that he can*	think
Mat Man has	2 eyes,	2 eyes,	2 eyes,	*(repeat)*	2 eyes,	*(repeat)*	see
Mat Man has	1 nose,	1 nose,	1 nose,		1 nose,		smell
Mat Man has	1 mouth,	1 mouth,	1 mouth,		1 mouth,		eat
Mat Man has	2 ears,	2 ears,	2 ears,		2 ears,		hear
Mat Man has	1 body,	1 body,	1 body,		1 body,	To hold what is inside	heart, lungs, stomach
Mat Man has	2 arms,	2 arms,	2 arms,		2 arms,	So that he can*	reach
Mat Man has	2 hands,	2 hands,	2 hands,		2 hands,	*(repeat)*	clap
Mat Man has	2 legs,	2 legs,	2 legs,		2 legs,		stand
Mat Man has	2 feet,	2 feet,	2 feet,		2 feet,		walk

* Wait for your children to respond. Add extra verses when you add new accessories. Your children may call out other body functions (feet= run, kick, dance). Encourage this while keeping the song/activity moving along.

19

Mat Man™ Pattern

Instructions:
Use these patterns to make body parts with colorful paper. Laminate for durability.

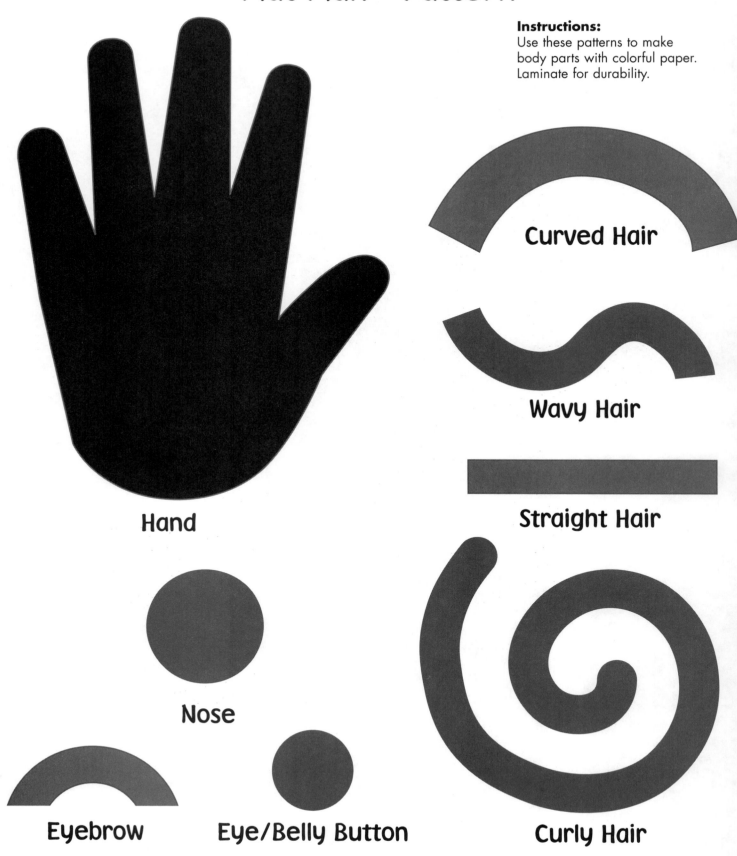

Hand

Curved Hair

Wavy Hair

Straight Hair

Nose

Curly Hair

Eyebrow

Eye/Belly Button

20

Mat Man™ Before and After

4 Year Old—Same Day

4 Year Old—Same Day

5 Year Old—9 Days Apart

Preparing for Capital Letters
Handwriting Readiness

This curriculum is not formal handwriting instruction. Preschoolers simply are not ready for either formal paper-pencil lessons or kindergarten type worksheets. Preschoolers need an informal readiness program that suits their developmental needs and abilities. Here's the difference between informal handwriting readiness and formal instruction:

INFORMAL	FORMAL
Informal Handwriting Readiness Structured, teacher selected activities	**Formal Handwriting Instruction** Structured, teacher directed lessons
When Pre-K and Kindergarten	**When** Kindergarten
Readiness Materials *Sing Along CD, Wood Pieces Set, Mat, Slate, Roll A Dough Letters™, Stamp and See Screen™* (Used for instruction)	**Readiness Materials** *Wood Pieces, Mat, Slate* (Used before paper/pencil instruction)
Writing Materials *Get Set for School™* workbook (a crayon book) Unlined paper, paper strips for "Name" Chalk, crayon	**Writing Materials** *Letters and Numbers for Me* workbook (crayon & pencil) Lined paper Chalk, crayon, pencil
Child develops pre-handwriting skills Attention Behavior Language Imitation Stop/start Fine motor	**Child learns handwriting** How to hold a pencil correctly Form capital and lowercase letters, numbers Write simple words and sentences Develop top to bottom, left to right orientation for reading/writing

The informal handwriting program prepares children to hold a crayon, to color and draw, and to imitate a few capitals and numbers. These beginning writing skills prepare a child to do well in a formal handwriting program.

Informal or Formal?
All young children should participate in readiness because the activities promote effective learning. Readiness activities appeal to the children's varied learning styles. The hands-on letter play also offers social and motor skills benefits. This prepares children for formal handwriting instruction. Even in kindergarten, do not begin formal instruction until children:

1. Have established hand dominance
2. Know simple size and shape concepts for big line/little line, big curve/little curve
3. Can hold a crayon with the fingers placed correctly
4. Have a satisfactory level of attention, cognitive skill and cooperation
5. Can imitate a vertical line, horizontal line, circle and cross

Handwriting Readiness, cont.

Readiness Level 1—Preparing Young Children

This early level invites everyone's participation. Play the CD in the background so that you and the children become familiar with the songs and activities. Soon they'll be singing the ABC's, counting legs on animals, and making Mat Man™. They'll use wood pieces to build letters on letter cards and mats. The social interaction and language aspects of these activities make them worthwhile for children at all levels.

Readiness Level 2—Hands-On Letter Play

This level focuses on developing fine motor skills and beginning letter skills. Show children how to hold and use a crayon to aim and scribble, and to color pictures and shapes in the *Get Set for School*™ workbook. At the same time, they'll continue to develop beginning letter skills through play. They'll roll out "snakes" to make Roll–A–Dough™ Letters. They'll stamp and trace letters with the Stamp and See Screen™.

Readiness Level 3—Crayon Skills

Now children begin writing. Continue to use the "Pick up a Crayon" song to be sure they're holding the crayon correctly. Continually demonstrate and supervise. Your modeling is so important at this stage. Use the slate "Wet–Dry–Try" activity just before you introduce the "crayon stroke" letters in the *Get Set for School*™ workbook. The "Wet–Dry–Try" activity directly teaches correct orientation and formation habits. Your children will know how to make the letters before they write! Show children how to write their names.

Where Do You Start Your Letters?

Here's a song. You know the tune; it's "If You're Happy and You Know It." But the words are different. They say, "Where Do You Start Your Letters?" Sing this song so often that your children will sing it at home and in the family car. Here's why. Parents listen. Parents are the first and most important teachers. It's parents who show children how to make letters. With this song, you are actually teaching the parents how to help their children. If they know that letters should start at the top, parents will model that for their children by singing the song. Children who start letters at the top learn to print automatically with speed and neatness. Children who start some letters at the bottom have to think about where to start. They aren't able to write automatically.

Gather Materials

CD Player and *Get Set for School*™ Sing Along CD

Directions

1. Teacher plays the CD track #1 and/or sings the song "Where Do Your Start Your Letters?"
2. Teacher demonstrates the song's motions, pointing to the top and later positions.
3. Children sing and imitate the teacher.

Where Do You Start Your Letters?

Tune: If You're Happy and You Know It

Where do you start your letters? At the top! Where do you start your letters? At the top!
If you want to start a letter, then you better, better, better, remember to start it at the top!
Is this the top, top, top? (Teacher leads by pointing to the floor) No it's the bottom!
Is this the top, top, top? (Teacher leads by pointing to the waist) No it's the middle!
Is this the top, top, top? (Teacher leads by pointing above head in the air.) Yes, it's the top, top, top!
Where do you start your letters? At the top!

Suggested Activity

- Divide class into two groups: One group sings to ask the question. The other group answers.

Capitals with Letter Cards

Building Capitals with Letter Cards

Teach children how to place wood pieces on the cards. Do one to three capitals each session. Use this lesson plan for F as a general guide.

Gather Materials

Capital Letter Cards
Wood Pieces

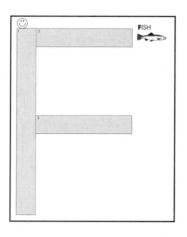 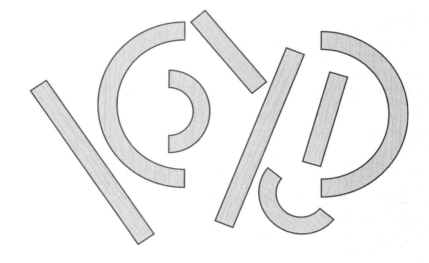

Directions

1. Place F card in front of child.
2. Point to the letter card. Say, "This is F. F starts at the ☺. This word is FISH. FISH begins with F."
   I'm putting the big line right here, under the ☺. Now, I'm getting a little line to put at the top. There it is.
   Now, I'm getting another little line to put at the middle. I made F."
3. Remove the pieces.

Tips for Teachers

- When working with a group of children, each child will have a different letter. Supervise to be sure the pieces are placed in the correct order. Help the children notice the number "1" on the card and then select and place that piece. Follow the numbers to complete each letter correctly.
- When working individually, you may teach planning skills by having the child gather the needed pieces first. Ask, "What do you need to make F?" First, you need…a big line. How many? One! Get one big line. Then you need… a little line. How many? Two! Get two little lines. You're ready!
- By spreading out the pieces randomly, you provide a figure–ground discrimination activity. Choosing the correct piece (figure) from the assortment (ground) develops visual discrimination.
- Placing each piece requires fine motor control and spatial (position) awareness. You may assist by placing the piece beside the card the way it will be used. Or you may place the piece, take it away and then let the child try.
- Use cards to encourage alphabet awareness. Give each child a card. Have children hold the cards up as the letters are called. Or have children line up alphabetically as the letters are called out.

Building Capitals with Letter Cards Help Children Develop

- **Letter Name/Sound Association**—Naming F, associating FISH with F and F sound
- **Visual Perception**—Part to whole association, figure ground discrimination
- **Sequence and Organization**—Placing wood pieces in order

Pre-writing and Language with Letter Cards

Match with Letter Cards

This side of the card has four beginning activities to teach letter awareness and same/different discrimination. Use this lesson plan for F as a general guide.

Gather Materials

Capital Letter Cards

Directions

Row 1. Capital letters made with wood pieces

Show children how to point to the first letter. Then demonstrate pointing to each letter in turn; looking for the one that matches. For example: Show the card. Say, "This page is about the letter F." Point to F. Say, "The first letter is F. Let's find another F."

Point to D. Ask, "Is this F?…No, no, no. This is D. D is different."
Point to E. Ask, "Is the F?…No, no, no. This is E. E is different."
Point to F. Ask, "Is the F?…Yes! This is F. It is the same letter."

Row 2. Pictures/words that begin with the same capital letter

Show children how to point to the first picture/word. Then demonstrate pointing to each picture/word in turn; looking for the one that matches. Point to FISH. Say, "This is a fish. FISH Starts with F. Let's find another fish."

Point to FOX. Ask, "Is this a FISH? No, no, no. This is a FOX."
Point to FISH. Ask, "Is this a FISH? Yes! This is a FISH. It matches."
Point to FAN. Ask, "Is this a FISH? No, no, no. This is a FAN."

Row 3. Capital letters made with chalk on slates

Find the capital letter that matches the first one.

Row 4. Printed capital and lowercase letters

Find the capital letter that matches the first one.

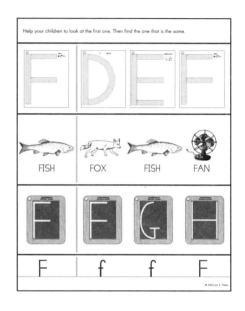

Tips for Teachers

- For children who don't know letters, just do the activity as if you're reading to the child. Encourage participation by following the child's lead.
- Avoid saying "a" or "an" before a letter name. It's confusing to hear "This is a B." Simply say, "This is B."
- Say, "Yes!" enthusiastically and nod your head. Or say, "No, no, no" in a cheerful way (like refusing dessert) and shake your head. Children will imitate this.
- The pictures promote left to right directionality. See how they face! Move your finger across each row from left to right and encourage children to imitate this.

The Pre-writing and Language Activity Helps Children Develop

- **Letter Name**—Letter name for F and f
- **Letter/Word Association**—Associating F with the FOX, FISH, FAN and the F sound
- **Same/Different Concepts**—Identifying same/different pictures and letters
- **Important Habits**—Using a page right side up, from top to bottom and left to right
- **Upper/Lower Letter Discrimination**—Difference between F and f

Build Capitals on the Mat

Teach children how to make capital letters on the HWT Mat. Unlike the letter cards, the mat does not have a letter printed on it. It is simply a bright blue fabric mat (like a mouse pad) with a yellow ☺ in the top left corner.

Gather Materials

Wood Pieces
Mat (1 per student)

Directions

1. Demonstrate how to form the letter piece by piece. (To see the stroke formation sequence, see page 99.)
2. Teach in a top–to–bottom, left–to–right order.
3. Tell your students to imitate how you make the letter.

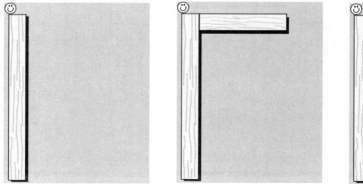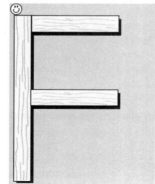

Tips for Teachers

- When building letters with a group, sit facing your students and build your letters upside down so the students will imitate you correctly.
- After success with the mat, teach students with the HWT Slate.

Building Letters on the HWT Mat Helps Children Develop

- **Letter Recognition**—Letter name for each letter
- **Organization**—What pieces are needed to make each letter
- **Directionality**—Top to bottom, left to right formation habits
- **Sequencing**—Making each letter step–by–step
- **Listening Skills/Imitation**—Following teacher directions and demonstrations
- **Sound/Letter Association**—Sound of each letter

26

HWT Roll-A-Dough Letters™

Roll Letters with Me!

Help children form capital letters out of dough. This activity helps children build strength in their fingers and hands while learning capital letter recognition.

Gather Materials

> HWT Roll–A–Dough™ Tray
> HWT Dough
> HWT Roll–A–Dough™ Letter Cards

Directions

1. Teacher shows how to roll dough (like making a rope or a snake).
2. Children imitate.
3. Teacher shows how to cut and place dough pieces to form a letter.
   (Use the letter card or just the tray.)
4. Children imitate.

Tips for Teachers

- To see the stroke formation sequence, see page 99.
- Use the HWT Roll-A-Dough™ tray for more sensory experiences with letters. Put shaving cream, sand, pudding, or finger paint in the tray. Then have the child "write" the capital letter with a finger.

Roll-A-Dough™ Letters Help Children Develop

- **Fine Motor Skills/Strength**—Rolling and pinching the dough develops the hands
- **Letter Recognition**—Naming the letter
- **Size/Position**—Judging length of the dough piece; Putting pieces on the card or the tray
- **Sensory Exploration**—Multiple sensory experiences help children learn using their senses

Stamp and See Screen™

Making Letters on the Stamp and See Screen™

Children learn how to make the capital letters step–by–step. The teacher shows how to stamp the pieces in the correct position and sequence. Later children may use the magnetic chalk to write the letter on the screen.

Gather Materials

Stamp and See Screen™
Magnetic big line, little line, big curve, little curve

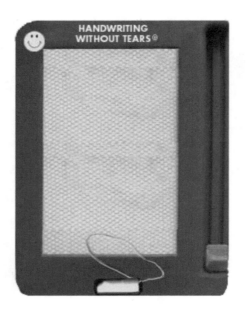  

Directions

1. Teacher stamps the first piece on the screen and then erases it.
2. Children imitate.
3. Teacher stamps the complete letter, step–by–step and then erases it.
4. Children imitate.
5. Children use the magnetic chalk to trace the letter and then they erase it.
6. Children make letter from memory using the pieces or the magnetic chalk.

Tips for Teachers

- Don't erase the screen too quickly. Allow ample time for the student to study the screen.
- Play mystery letter game: First person stamps a big line on the left edge of screen. The other person makes a mystery letter by stamping pieces on the right side. The first person doesn't know what the letter will be.
- Use cards from the Roll-A-Dough Letters™. Choose a card, place it on the magnetic screen, have your student trace over the letter with the magnetic chalk. Remove the card to see the letter on the screen. Retrace now.

Stamp and See Screen™ Helps Children Develop

- **Letter Recognition**—Naming the letter
- **Organization**—Choosing the pieces to make the letter
- **Directionality**—Top to bottom, left to right habits
- **Sequencing**—Making letters step–by–step in correct order
- **Visual Perception**—Visual memory of each step as it's erased
- **Listening Skills/Imitation**—Following teacher directions/demonstrations
- **Sound/Letter Association**—Letter sound for each letter

HWT Slate Chalkboard

Teach Capitals with Wet-Dry-Try

The Wet–Dry–Try method is a sensory strategy to teach the strokes for capital letters. Wet–Dry–Try appeals to all learning styles (visual, auditory, tactile, and kinesthetic) and it is lots of fun.

Gather Materials

Slate (1 per child)
Little chalk pieces
Little sponge pieces
Paper towel
Bowl of water

Teacher's Part

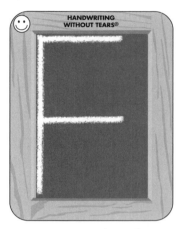

Demonstrate correct letter formation.

Student's Part

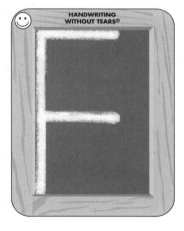

WET
Wet tiny sponge. Squeeze out. With damp sponge, trace over the letter like the teacher demonstrated. Wet index finger. Trace letter again with your wet finger.

DRY
Use a small piece of paper towel to trace the letter dry. Repeat two or three times.

TRY
Now, try writing the letter with a small piece of chalk.

Tips for Teachers

- Use consistent words to describe the strokes (big line, little line, big curve, little curve).
- Use very small pieces of sponge and chalk—this helps develop the pencil grip.
- Squeeze the sponge well or the letter will be too wet.
- This works best one–on–one or in centers with five or fewer students.
- To use this activity with the whole class you must pre–mark each student slate with the capital letter (so they have a correct model to wet) and then demonstrate once for everyone.

HWT Slate Chalkboard, cont.

Teach Capitals with the HWT Slate
Teacher demonstrates each new capital letter on the slate. Children imitate.

Gather Materials
Slate (1 per child)
Little chalk pieces
Eraser

Directions
Demonstrate R
1. Put chalk in the starting corner ☺.
2. Big line down.
3. Jump back up to the starting corner.
4. Little curve to the middle.
5. Little line slides down.

Teach on the Slate
Your teaching will vary according to the number of children and slates.
When teacher and students each have a slate:
1. Teacher demonstrates the first step, saying, "I put the chalk in the starting corner."
2. Students imitate that and continue to imitate step by step on their own slates.
When teacher and student share one slate:
1. Teacher demonstrates on the front of the slate. Turn slate over.
2. Student imitates on the back of the slate

Tips for Teachers
- The ☺ is the cue to the top. In a large class, students are happy to check each other to be sure all the slates are right side up.
- The ☺ prevents reversals. When children start F E D P B R N K L with a big line down from the ☺, the line will be on the left side of the slate and the next part will always be on the right side.
- The wood frame gives children an edge so that their chalk lines are neat and straight. Their letters are uniform in size and shape.
- The frame and ☺ give children a frame of reference. They can think about the slate and it will help them remember how to make letters.

My Name Starts with...

Sign in Please!

You may remember an old TV show where the guests signed in. This adaptation is fun and develops many ABC skills. Children sign in alphabetically.

Preparation

1. Prepare blackboard with a wide "stop" line near the bottom. (A blackboard is best, but you may use a white board.)
2. Break chalk into small 1/2" pieces to encourage correct pinch.

Directions

1. Teacher prints A.
   - Write A up high, but reachable for children.
   - Teach A and each letter that follows as you write.
   - Use consistent words as you demonstrate (A = big line, big line, and little line).
2. Teacher asks, "Whose name begin with A?" **Adam**!
3. Adam comes to the board and you introduce him saying:
   "This is...(children say **Adam**)."
   "Adam starts with...(children say **A**)."
   "In Adam's name, the A makes the sound (children make the A sound)."
4. Adam signs in by making a big line down from A. He stops on the line. Continue with each letter. Children sign in alphabetically. David is at the board now.

What Skills Are We Developing?

- **Top to bottom** habit
- **Stopping** on a line
- **Names** of capital letters and classmates
- **Phonics**—Sounds of letters are easy to do with classmates' names
- **Correct letter formation**—Children learn by watching and hearing the teacher.
- **Big line, little line, big curve, and little curve**—Children learn the names for the parts of each letter.
- **Alphabetical order**—Children quickly learn their place in the alphabet. They guess which letter is next and watch to see if they're right. They look for classmates' names too.
- **Left to right** sequencing
- **Social skills** for school—This is a fun way to learn to listen, be in front of the class, follow directions, and take turns. Children develop poise and a sense of belonging.
- **Pencil Grip**—The small pieces of chalk encourage correct grip.
- **Number Concepts**—Counting and comparing

Variation: You can change how children sign in to teach other skills.
- **Horizontal Line Skills**—Underline letter from left to right.
- **Circle Skills**—Circle the letter by starting at the top with a C stroke.

Developmental Stages in Writing Readiness

Using a writing tool correctly requires instruction. Correct grips need to be taught. Awkward grips just happen. How children hold the crayon, chalk or pencil depends on their developmental stage, the writing tool being used, and the instruction the students receive. Here is a general guide of how children develop with proper instruction and practice.

2 Year Old—scribble mark, vertical line, horizontal line

Writing hand/arm: Child uses all fingers to hold crayon in palm of the hand. Arm is in the air expressing anticipation.

Helping hand/arm: Has no purposeful use.

Present skill: Child makes random contact with the paper.

Next skill: Show child how to make scribbles, lines down and lines across.

3 Year Old—circle, cross

Writing hand/arm: Child uses all fingers to hold crayon in the palm of the hand. Arm is down on the table, but not well planted.

Helping hand/arm: Child is just starting to use the helping hand.

Present skill: Copies lines down and lines across

Next skill: Show child how to make a circle and cross.

Developing Motor Skills for Twos and Threes

Outside—Use playground equipment, swings, slides, big push and riding toys, sandbox play, and balls.

Inside—Use building blocks to teach controlled release. Nesting toys use both sides of the body. Toy trains, animals, and cars teach manipulating skills. Puzzles teach visual discrimination and placing skills. Pictures encourage pointing. Avoid high tech toys and stick with the classics.

Daily Life—Encourage undressing (easier) and dressing, washing hands and brushing teeth. Eating small food pieces gives practice picking up very little things. Have children help with simple take out and put away tasks.

Developmental Stages in Writing Readiness, cont.

4 Year Old—square, triangle

Writing hand/arm: Mature grasp begins to emerge (using thumb with 1 or 2 fingers). Notice the elbow. It's up. This is "arm" writing. The hand moves freely in the air.

Helping hand/arm: Child starts to deliberately hold the paper.

Present skill: Copies line down, line across, circle and cross

Next skill: Show this child how to make a square and a triangle. Show the child how to trace letters and numbers. Help with holding a crayon. Use stencils. Holding the stencil still helps develop the helping hand. Continue with free exploration.

5 Year Old—diamond

Writing hand/arm: Use mature grasp. This is "hand" writing. The hand rests on the paper.

Helping hand/arm: Child purposely uses the hand to hold and place the paper.

Present skill: Copies a cross, circle, square and triangle

Next skill: Child begins to independently draw circle, square, and triangle. Show this child how to draw a diamond. Show this child how to write letters and numbers. Help with holding a crayon if needed. Encourage drawing.

Developing Motor Skills for Fours and Fives

Outside—Continue previous activities. Add simple games and building projects.

Inside—Continue previous activities. Finger painting, easel work, and drawing with little pieces of chalk or crayon develop coordination and holding habits. Finger–plays, music and imitating build body awareness. Play dough, toys with small pieces, and simple crafts like bead stringing develop fine motor skills.

Daily Life—Continue previous activities. Add more helping tasks that use precise fine motor control; pouring, spreading, setting table.

Teaching Shapes

Build, Color, Trace, Sing and Draw Shapes Together
Learning Shapes doesn't have to be boring. Use these fun, easy ideas for teaching shapes.

Build Shapes with Wood Pieces
See this guide: pages 6–14 to learn about Wood Pieces.

Directions
1. Demonstrate making shapes on the floor.
> Circles = 2 big curves or 2 little curves
> Crosses = 2 big lines or 2 little lines
> Squares = 4 big lines or 4 little lines
> Triangles = 3 big lines or 3 little lines
> Rectangle = 2 big lines and 2 little lines
2. Ask children to hand you the pieces as you build the shapes.
3. Always start the circles with a "C."
4. Leave your models on the floor for children to copy.

Color Shapes in the workbook
See this guide: pages 44-48 for specific instructions.

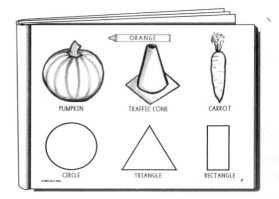

Directions
1. Teach the name of the shape.
2. Finger trace the shapes.
3. Help the children choose the right color crayon.
4. Show children how to move the crayon to follow the shapes.

Trace Shapes in the workbook
See this guide pages: 51–56, 58–68, 70–74 for specific instructions.

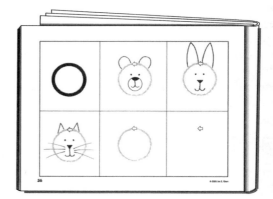

Directions
1. Teach these pages as they come in the workbook.
2. Teach the names of the shapes.
3. Demonstrate crayon tracing.
4. Show children how to change the shape into a picture.

Sing and Draw Shapes with the CD Track 17
See this guide page: 90. Use an easel, flip chart or board for this activity.

Directions
1. Teach these shapes as they come in the workbook.
2. Let children watch you change shapes into pictures
3. Let children imitate you. Do not use the CD for this.
4. Make very simple drawings step by step for them to imitate

34   Note: This activity is designed to give children confidence so that they'll draw more freely.

Fine Motor Skills and Strength

Developing fine motor skills is one of the most important parts of a preschool teacher's job. Here are new and familiar activities for encouraging fine motor skills.

Finger–Plays

Use familiar finger–plays Try new finger–plays from the HWT Sing Along CD.
- "The Ant, The Bug, and The Bee" (see page 43)
- "Spiders Love to Party" (see page 89)
- "Five Fingers Play" (see page 87)
- "Ten Fingers" (see below)

Ten Little Fingers

I have ten little fingers and they all belong to me
I can make them do things, Just you wait and see
I can wiggle them high, And wiggle them low
I can push them on the floor, And stretch them just so
They can make little Os, If I touch them together
They can even make a cup, To catch rain in rainy weather
I can stretch them out wide, Or close them real tight
I might just fold them quietly, When I sleep at night

Suggested Activity

- Use this song to warm up the hands. This song helps children to move their fingers in a variety of ways. Use as a finger–play any time of day.

Toys

We live in a world of technology. Toys are different today than they were several years ago. They light up, talk, and play music at the push of a button. Even many "educational" toys do not give the child anything to do beyond pushing buttons. Be picky about the toys you choose. Select toys that require children to use hand skills to move pieces, manipulate parts or snap things together.

Easel Activities

Vertical surfaces are great for developing hand skills. Other vertical surfaces include mirrors, windows, walls (tub walls too!), and refrigerators. The best part about a vertical surface is that children create their own working space at just the right height! When a child's arms and hands are positioned upward working against gravity, they are building strength in the shoulders and arms. Also, a child's wrist is forced into a neutral position, which is the position that is used later, when the child begins to write. For more ideas on easel activities turn to page 5.

Playing with Dough Letters

Preschoolers love to play with dough. Most enjoy touchy/feely sensory experiences. Use the HWT Roll–A–Dough Letters™ to encourage fine motor skills and hand strength. For directions on this activity turn to page 27.

Playground Play

Did you know that most children's upper body strength and motor coordination develop through play? The use of playground equipment is a great way to help a child develop the strength and coordination required for fine motor skills. Some children may never have the opportunity to use playground equipment. Allow time in your day for children to experience the benefits of monkey bars, swings and other great playground equipment.

Educating Parents

Parents are a child's most important teacher. Parents love to help their children learn. Educate parents about preschool activities by sending home the parent articles in the back of this guide. It's amazing what good habits can be taught to children when we all work together.

Hold On...You Have to Teach Grip

Research shows that close to 50% of three year olds have the fine motor ability to hold a small crayon correctly.* But the correct grip has to be taught to children. You can put an end to awkward or even fisted pencil grips by using direct teaching and certain strategies. Young children are pliable—they can be molded gently into good habits. Here are strategies for you to use when teaching a correct crayon grip.

Handedness
If a child is truly undecided by the time handwriting training begins, choose the hand that is more skilled to be the writing hand. Without a "dominant" hand, experience and training is divided between two hands and children develop nearly equal hand skills. But they are not as skilled with one hand as their peers who have given a dominant hand more training. To determine which hand is most skilled, take the "functional" approach. A teacher, parent, and an occupational therapist (if available) should observe the child. Watch how child colors, draws, writes, zips a jacket, eats, etc. This will allow all of the observers to determine which hand appears the more skilled. Once a dominant hand is determined, encourage the child to use the more skilled hand during writing tasks. Placing utensils, crayons or chalk on that side will help.

Little Crayons/Little Pencils
With all the fun writing tools available today it's hard to decide what is age appropriate. The best tool for Pre-K children is the crayon. Crayons create a natural resistance and build strength in the hand. Little pieces of crayon are perfect for little hands because they require children to use their fingertips correctly. They prepare the hand for using a good pencil grip. Sort little bits of crayon by color in bowls. A lazy susan makes it even more fun. Use markers, colored pencils, etc. in moderation. Don't promote pencil use very much. Children will get plenty of practice using pencils in Kindergarten when their hands are ready. When moving a child to a pencil, use a golf size pencil. Children will do better with a short pencil that's in proportion with the size of their hand. Avoid fat "primary pencils." They are too heavy and too long for little hands.

Weinraub, D.L. (1999). *The Effects of The Use of Broken Crayons Upon Grasp Development In Conjunction with Occupational Therapy.* Unpublished master's thesis, Touro College, Far Rockaway, NY.

Demonstrate Grip
The time to teach proper grip is when a child becomes interested in coloring. Show children how to hold their crayons correctly by showing them finger placement and modeling a correct grip.

Standard and Alternate Grip
The standard grip, also called the "tripod grip" uses three fingers to hold the crayon or pencil. The thumb is bent, the index finger is pointing to the tip of the crayon and the crayon rests on the side of the middle finger. The last two fingers are curled in the palm and give the hand stability.

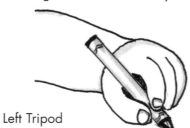
Left Tripod

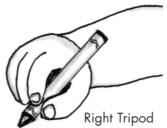
Right Tripod

An alternative grip, called the quadropod grip (four fingers) is another way children may hold their crayon. The thumb is bent, the index and middle finger point to the tip of the crayon and the crayon rests on the ring finger. This grip is efficient and should not be considered something that needs to be corrected.

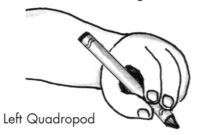
Left Quadropod

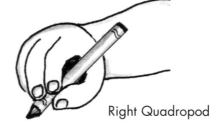
Right Quadropod

Research states that close to 50% of 3-year-olds are already using a mature tripod grasp.*
*Schneck, C.M., & Henderson , A. (1990). Descriptive analysis of the developmental progression of grip position for pencil and crayon in nondysfunctional children. *American Journal of Occupational Therapy, 44,* 893–900.
Tseng, M.H. (1998). Development of pencil grip position in preschool children. *Occupational Therapy Journal of Research, 18,* 207–224.
Yakimishyn, J.E. & Magill-Evans, J. (2002). Comparisons among tools, surface orientation, and pencil grasp for children 23 months of age. *American Journal of Occupational Therapy, 56,* 564–572.

Hold On...You Have to Teach Grip, cont.

Teach the Correct Pencil Grip in Three Easy Steps
This step–by–step technique is a great way to develop a correct pencil grip or to fix an awkward one. The trick is that you teach the grip in three separate stages. At first, you help children pick up the crayon and hold it correctly. That's all. Next, you show them how to aim the crayon and scribble on paper. Then, you teach them how to make deliberate strokes.

Pick Up (Remember they don't write at this stage. Don't even have paper on the table.)
Tell the children to pick up the crayon and hold it in the air! Help them place their fingers correctly. Then say, "Wow, that is just right! Let's take the crayons for a ride in the air." Now tell them to gently drop the crayons. Do it again. Sing the "Crayon Song" when you do this activity. Continue with this activity until children can automatically pick up and hold the crayon correctly.

Aim and Scribble (Use blank paper with a dot like this • or start the *Get Set for School*™ workbook.)
Tell children to aim the crayon and put it on the dot or star. The little finger side of the "crayon hand" should rest on the paper. Some children will need help in putting the crayon hand down. Don't forget the helping hand. It has to be flat and resting on the paper. Now it's time to scribble. Don't lift the crayon or hand, just wiggle and scribble. The beauty of this step is that children develop their crayon grip and finger control without being critical of how the writing or drawing looks.

Color/Trace/Draw (Use *Get Set for School*™ workbook.)
Have children pick up a crayon and use it for workbook pages or free drawing. Continue using previous steps as needed to reinforce the correct habits. This will get your students off to a wonderful start.

Pencil Grips
At a young age, children are motivated to learn new skills. If a child is holding a crayon or small pencil incorrectly, demonstrate the proper grip for them and try the techniques described above or on page 95. Avoid using pencil grips or any other type of adaptive writing device for preschoolers. A physical device cannot substitute for a child being taught how to hold the crayon or pencil. Pencil grips are for older children who find them helpful.

Introduce Fingers
Children need to know their fingers so that they can follow your directions. Start by naming the fingers that hold the crayon. Here is how to introduce them:
          Thumb—Everyone, hold up your thumb. Say "Hi" to your thumb. "Hi thumb."
          Pointer—Hold up your pointer finger. Wiggle it around. Say "Hi" to pointer finger. "Hi pointer."
          Middle—Hold up middle finger next to pointer. Middle finger is taller than the pointer finger.
               We call him "Tall Man" because he is the tallest finger.
        Now say, "Your fingers have very important jobs to do. I'm going to teach you a song so you can
             remember their jobs."

Crayon Song

Pick up a crayon, Pick up a crayon, This is easy to do
Pick up a crayon, Pick up a crayon, I just tell my fingers what to do
My thumb is bent, Pointer points to the tip, Tall Man uses his side
I tuck my last two fingers in and take them for a ride

Now I'm holding it just right, But not too tight, Every finger knows what to do
And now I have a big surprise, A big surprise for you
Let's drop it and do it again!

NOTE: Use the CD just to learn the tune. Then use the song without the CD while teaching. As you are singing the song, it's very important to walk around the room and position children's fingers for them correctly on the crayon. It will take several repetitions before children will pick up the habit naturally.

The Helper Hand

The Role of the Helper Hand
The focus has been on the writing hand, but the helping hand is important too. The helping hand positions and holds the paper. The helping hand helps maintain good posture while children write. To develop handwriting skill efficiently, children need to use the helping hand consistently.

Developing Dominant and Helping Hands
Some activities, like eating with a spoon, use just one hand. They are unilateral activities. Other activities use two hands and are called bilateral activities. Some bilateral activities, like pushing a cart, or holding on to a swing, use the hands in the same way. Neither hand develops superior skill. But other bilateral activities, like stringing beads, use the hands for different purposes. The dominant hand develops superior skill while the other hand is used as a holding hand. These activities are good for both hands. It is important to provide bilateral activities that train a child to use a helping hand. These activities prepare for handwriting by requiring them to use the helping hand. Here are a few:
- Holding a container of bubble soap while dipping the wand and blowing bubbles
- Holding a bowl and stirring
- Holding beads and stringing them
- Holding a funnel and spooning sand into the funnel
- Holding a box of something and taking things out
- Holding a flower and picking petals

Encouranging Children to Use the Helper Hand
1. HWT suggests these activities that require using the helping hand:
   - Wood Pieces—Hold a wood piece and rub it with the other hand.
   - Slate—Hold a slate steady on the table and write on it with chalk.
   - Stencils, shapes, and rulers—Hold them steady with one hand while marking with the other.
   - Hand tracing—Hold one hand flat while the other hand traces around it.

2. When preparing children for writing, be sure to tell them to hold the paper with a flat helping hand. Keeping the hand flat helps children stay relaxed when they write.

3. If children ignore the helping hand when coloring or starting to write, try this:
   Give the helping hand a name. Ask the child to choose a name, one that starts with the same letter as their name. Then talk directly to the hand (not the child) and call the hand by the new name. Tell the helping hand to help the child. Tell the hand to hold the paper. Children think it's funny when you talk to the hand. They don't get embarrassed because it's the helping hand, not them, that's being corrected.

Use Your Oven Rack
You may never have thought that your oven rack could be so handy. You can help a child learn vertical and horizontal lines by using your oven rack. Plop the rack on a large sheet of paper, hand the child a crayon and let them make lines back and forth. By holding the rack with their other hand, they are getting practice using their helping hand for stabilization.

Readiness Made Easy
Developmental Teaching Order

The readiness activities have prepared your children for success with capital letters. Now, they're ready to begin coloring, tracing lines, shapes, letters and numbers in *Get Set for School.*™ The workbook lessons are planned to follow a developmentally based teaching order.

Begin with Crayon Skills

The "Aim and Scribble" pages are unique. These pages are used while teaching beginning crayon skills: picking up, holding, aiming/placing and moving the crayon. It's so nice for beginners to just land on a star or firefly and make it shine by wiggling and scribbling. Children have fun learning basic crayon skills with these pictures.

"Fill In" Coloring—Colors, Pictures, and Shapes

"Fill in" coloring is next. Children learn to move the crayon more deliberately now. The pictures and shapes encourage children to stay within a certain area and use back and forth, up and down or side-to-side strokes. The pictures and shapes are easy to color. They use bold outlines and avoid any tiny details or overlapping parts. While using these pages, the teacher helps children learn the names of all the pictures, colors and shapes. Some are new! Children begin to think of shapes as they relate to objects or pictures. "Fill in" coloring will continue throughout the book. Coloring is such an important and valuable activity.

 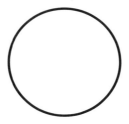

Benefits of Coloring

It's a joy watching children color. Children generally love to color because it's fun and it gives them freedom to be creative. Developmentally, children will color broadly over a picture and then as their skill develops, they will grade their movements into smaller more refined strokes. Because coloring is such a common activity, we forget the great benefits coloring has for developing coordination, grip and strength. By observing how a child colors, the teacher can determine handwriting readiness. The following skills can be observed:

- Attention
- Crayon Grip
- Control
- Posture/Strength/Endurance
- Use of the Helping Hand

Help children color:

1. Choose easy to color, appealing pictures.
2. Help children hold the crayon.
   (See page 36 for teaching crayon grip.)
3. Demonstrate coloring on a separate page.
   - Side to side (horizontal) strokes
   - Up and down strokes
   - Little circular motions
   - Staying in the lines or following the direction of the lines
4. Encourage children to draw on their pictures.

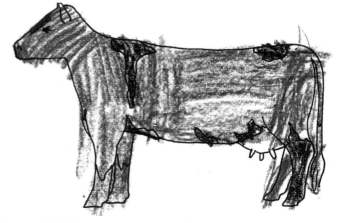

Generally, the shape of the picture will determine which stroke a child chooses to use. See the crayon stroke pattern on the cow above. If a child is unable to organize his/her stroke to accommodate the shape of the picture, encourage the child to color up/down as it is the easiest.

Developmental Teaching Order, cont.

Strokes—Pre-Strokes, Shapes, Letters, and Numbers

What's new is making deliberate single strokes with control. Some strokes are easier to write (developmentally) than others.* Children gradually develop their ability to copy forms in a very predictable order. The *Get Set for School*™ workbook teaches strokes to children based on the following order:

Children learn how to "steer" the crayon with pre-stroke pages. The pre-stroke pages are fun and give lots of practice moving the crayon. The "crayon stroke" lines may be traced over and over as children learn to make vertical, horizontal, curved or diagonal lines. These pages are appealing, easy to do and fun. They prepare children for correctly tracing and learning how to make shapes, letters and numbers. Crayon skills continue to be refined with coloring and children develop more control for starting and stopping strokes. Note: The HWT readiness activities (Easel, Mat Man, Build and Draw) develop skill, confidence and interest in drawing. Children are encouraged to add their own finishing touches and extra drawings to all the workbook pages.

Workbook Design

Get Set for School™ works because it is carefully designed for Pre–K children. It uses appropriate lessons, not kindergarten or first grade work. The hands on, multi-sensory activities lead right into the workbook pages. Even so, teachers decide when their students are ready to start the workbook and how they'll use the pages. Not all children need to use the pages in the same way. If children aren't ready to trace the letters and numbers, they can use the workbook as a picture book, a coloring and counting book. The workbook has been carefully designed to be child friendly and to promote learning and good habits. By design, you'll find *Get Set for School*™ is:

A Workbook that Sings

Get Set for School™ comes to life with 2003 Grammy winning artists Cathy Fink and Marcy Marxer. They bring music and that facilitates participation, rhythm and movement. Writing is the trace of movement! Therefore, moving before coloring, tracing, or drawing is great for children. Here's just one way we use music. Children sing "The Ant, The Bug and The Bee" song. They do the simple motions. Then on workbook pages 4 and 5 they color the ladybug red, the ant black and the bee yellow. They trace crayon strokes up, down and flying around. Later they'll count 6 ladybugs and 6 legs! Music and movement enhance learning, memory and workbook skills.

*Gesell, Arnold, and others. *The First Five Years of Life*. New York: Harper and Row. 1940.

Workbook Design, cont.

A Workbook that's Simple
The *Get Set for School*™ workbook, like all HWT workbooks, has simple black-and-white pages that are clean and clear. We deliberately avoid distracting background images, colored graphics, multicolored lines, and crowded pages. These "fancy" effects can create visual perceptual difficulties for children and distract them. Instead, the pages are simply black and white. They invite coloring. The pictures and shapes are large and easy to color. The letters and numbers are also large and easy to trace. They are consistently placed near the bottom of the page to make it easy for children to stop near the end of the page.

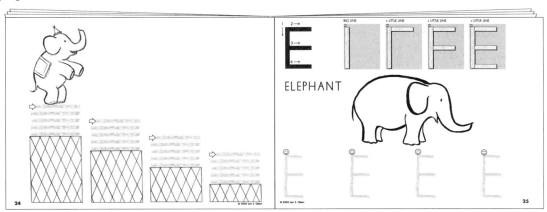

A Workbook with Consistent Words
Get Set for School™ uses consistent words to teach capital letters. First, through play and activities, children are taught the names for the Wood Pieces: **big line**, **big curve**, **little line**, and **little curve**. We say these words when we make letters with the wood pieces. For example, letter D is made with 1 big line and 1 big curve. The workbook letter pages illustrate this step by step. Simple, consistent words make it easy to learn letters. Saying the words out loud while tracing helps children understand how to make letters.

A Workbook with Unique "Crayon Strokes"
HWT has designed the unique gray "crayon stroke." After trying various tracing methods, we found that this is the easiest stroke for children to trace. Dot to dot letters don't work because children focus on the dots, just going from one dot to the next. They learn to follow dots, but they don't learn the strokes. Crayon strokes are seen as complete strokes. Children follow and learn the basic strokes easily. There is a surprise too. When children trace over the strokes, the underlying gray strokes disappear! The page shows just the child's letters or numbers. Children are so proud!

...with Easy Starts and Stops
The crayon stroke letters and numbers are easy to start. That's because each letter has a starting symbol to cue children where to put their crayon to start the letter. It may be a ☺ or an ⇨. To prepare, the children simply place the crayon on the starting icon and then follow the gray crayon stroke. All letters and numbers begin at the top. That's easy too. Stopping is easy too. The page stops! The letters are placed at the bottom of the page. Children know that they aren't supposed to write on the table. They see the page ending and they get ready to slow down and stop.

A Workbook that Counts!
Each number page has a related counting activity. Children make numbers 1—5 with fingers, wood pieces and the slate. They also color the picture and trace the crayon stroke numbers. Numbers 6—10 have pictures to count. The workbook pages for numbers 2, 4, 6, and 8 directly relate to songs on the Sing Along CD. All of this adds up to a successful experience for the child who'll be entering kindergarten.

Teaching with the Workbook
Crayon Skills

Night Sky—Aim and Scribble

Ask
Have you ever seen stars in the sky?
What color are they? What color is the moon?
Have you ever seen a firefly? When do fireflies come out?

Begin to look and learn
Let's find fireflies. (Point) Let's find stars. (Point)
Let's find the moon. (Point)

Color
Let's sing the "Crayon Song" (see page 36).
Let's color the moon yellow.

Demonstrate
Let's scribble stars. Put the crayon on the star. Scribble.
Let's scribble fireflies. Put the crayon on the firefly. Scribble.

Extra
Look at other pictures of fireflies.

Twinkle—Aim and Scribble

Ask
Do you sleep under a quilt? What color is it?
Have you ever seen stars in the sky? What color are they?

Begin to look and learn
Let's find the quilt. (Point) Let's find stars. (Point)
Let's find the moon. (Point)

Color
Let's color the quilt.

Demonstrate
Let's scribble stars. Put the crayon on the star. Scribble.

Extra
Sing "Twinkle, Twinkle Little Star."

Fireworks—Aim and Scribble

Ask
Have you ever seen fireworks? What color are they?
Do we see fireworks during the day or at night?

Begin to look and learn
Let's find fireworks. (Point) Let's find stars. (Point)
Let's find the children. (Point)

Color
Let's color the children.

Demonstrate
Let's scribble fireworks. Put the crayon on the star.

Extra
Look at pictures of fireworks.

42

Crayon Skills, cont.

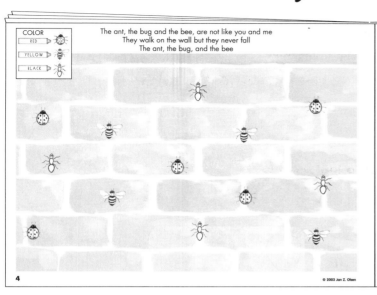

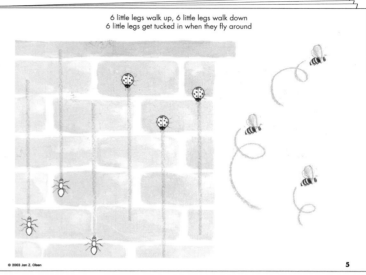

The Ant, The Bug, and The Bee

The ant, the bug, and the bee
Are not like you and me
They walk on the wall
But they never fall
The ant, the bug, and the bee

Six little legs walk up
Six little legs walk down
Six little legs get tucked in
When they fly around

The ant, the bug, and the bee
Are not like you and me
They walk on the wall
But they never fall
The ant, the bug, and the bee

Six little legs in the air
Six little legs on the tree
Six little legs go everywhere
But not on me!

Ask about insects
Have you ever seen ants? What color are they?
Have you ever seen ladybugs? What color are they?
Have you ever seen bees? What color are they?

Begin to look and learn
Play and sing the "The Ant, The Bug and The Bee" song (see above)
Let's find ants. (Point)
Let's find ladybugs. (Point)
Let's find the bees. (Point)

Color
Color the ants, the bugs, and the bees.

Demonstrate tracing
Let's trace lines up, down, and all around. Put the crayon on the ant. Line goes up.
Put the crayon on the ladybug. Line goes down. Put the crayon on the bee. Line goes all around.

Extra
Sing the song. Have the children put their hands together with three fingers up on each hand. Then crawl fingers up and down and all around. Fly around like bees.

Pictures, Colors, and Shapes

Pages 6–15 feature one color per page. Help the children color the crayons at the top of each page to show what color to use. They may skip from page to page, coloring what interests them. For all other pages, children choose colors freely.

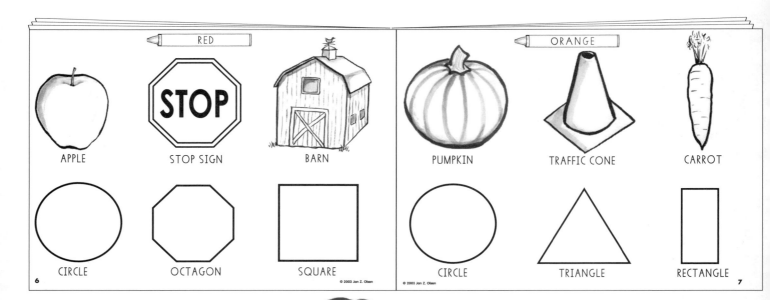

RED
APPLE   STOP SIGN   BARN
CIRCLE   OCTAGON   SQUARE
6   © 2003 Jan Z. Olsen

© 2003 Jan Z. Olsen   ORANGE
PUMPKIN   TRAFFIC CONE   CARROT
CIRCLE   TRIANGLE   RECTANGLE   7

Red

Ask about red
Can you find the crayon? (Point)
This crayon is going to be red.
Do you know anything that is red?

Begin to look and learn
Let's find the apple. (Point)
Let's find the stop sign. (Point)
Let's find the barn. (Point)
Let's find the circle. (Point)
Let's find the octagon. (Point)
Let's find the square. (Point)

Color
Let's Sing the "Crayon Song" (see page 36).
Color the apple, stop sign and barn red.
Color the shapes below red.

Demonstrate
Let's trace shapes. Put finger on shape and trace.

Extra
Point to red items in the room.

Orange

Ask about orange
Can you find the crayon? (Point)
This crayon is going to be orange.
Do you know anything that is orange?

Begin to look and learn
Let's find the pumpkin. (Point)
Let's find the traffic cone. (Point)
Let's find the carrot. (Point)
Let's find the circle. (Point)
Let's find the triangle. (Point)
Let's find the rectangle. (Point)

Color
Color the pumpkin, traffic cone, and carrot orange.
Color the shapes below orange.

Demonstrate
Let's trace shapes. Put finger on shape and trace.

Extra
Point to orange items in the room.
Have carrots for a snack.
Mix red and yellow paint to make orange.

Pictures, Colors, and Shapes, cont.

Help children pick up, hold, and move the crayon. Use the "Crayon Song," track 5 on the CD. On a separate paper, demonstrate how to move back and forth to do "fill in" coloring. Watching you helps children learn how to color.

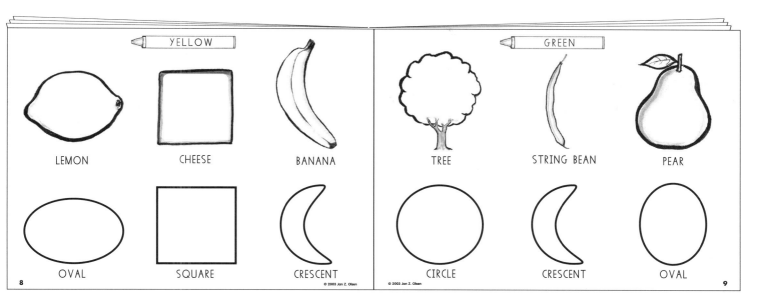

Yellow

Ask about yellow
Can you find the crayon? (Point)
This crayon is going to be yellow.
Do you know anything that is yellow?

Begin to look and learn
Let's find the lemon. (Point)
Let's find the cheese. (Point)
Let's find the banana. (Point)
Let's find the oval. (Point)
Let's find the square. (Point)
Let's find the crescent. (Point)

Color
Color the lemon, cheese, and banana yellow.
Color the shapes below yellow.

Demonstrate
Let's trace shapes. Put finger on shape and trace.

Extra
Point to yellow items in the room.
See who is wearing something yellow.

Green

Ask about green
Can you find the crayon? (Point)
This crayon is going to be green.
Do you know anything that is green?

Begin to look and learn
Let's find the tree. (Point)
Let's find the string bean. (Point)
Let's find the pear. (Point)
Let's find the circle. (Point)
Let's find the crescent. (Point)
Let's find the oval. (Point)

Color
Color the tree, string bean and pear green.
Color the shapes below green.

Demonstrate
Let's trace shapes. Put finger on shape and trace.

Extra
Point to green items in the room.
Mix blue and yellow to make green.
Eat green snacks.

Pictures, Colors, and Shapes, cont.

Help children make little circular strokes, by moving the crayon tip round and round. Show them how to rest the crayon hand with the little finger side of the hand on the page.

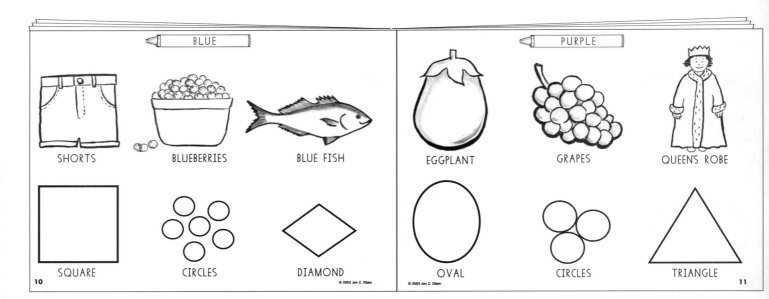

Blue

Ask about blue
Can you find the crayon? (Point)
This crayon is going to be blue.
Do you know anything that is blue?

Begin to look and learn
Let's find the shorts. (Point)
Let's find the blueberries. (Point)
Let's find the fish. (Point)
Let's find the square. (Point)
Let's find the little circles. (Point)
Let's find the diamond. (Point)

Color
Color the shorts, blueberries, and fish blue.
Color the shapes below blue.
Let's sing the "Crayon Song."
Lyrics and activities for this song are on page 37.

Demonstrate
Show how to color using little circular strokes.

Extra
Point to blue items in the room.
Eat blueberries for a snack.

Purple

Ask about purple
Can you find the crayon? (Point)
This crayon is going to be purple.
Do you know anything that is purple?

Begin to look and learn
Let's find the eggplant. (Point)
Let's find the grapes. (Point)
Let's find the queen's robe. (Point)
Let's find the oval. (Point)
Let's find the circles. (Point)
Let's find the triangle. (Point)

Color
Color the eggplant, grapes and queen's robe purple.
Color the shapes below.

Demonstrate
Show how to color using little circular strokes.

Extra
Point to purple items in the room.
Mix red and blue paint to make purple.
Eat purple grapes for a snack.

Pictures, Colors, and Shapes, cont.

These pages are structured to teach pictures, shapes and coloring skills. Be sure your children also enjoy many unstructured art activities. See page 5 for suggestions.

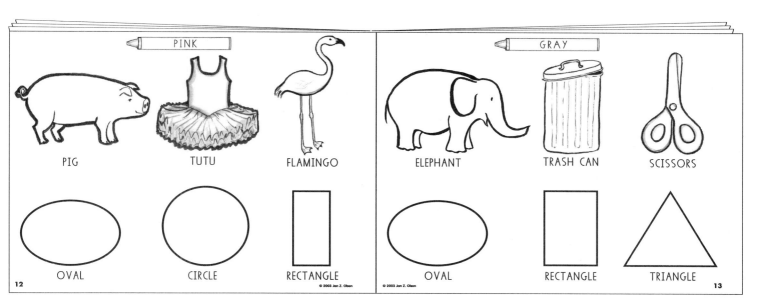

PINK

PIG   TUTU   FLAMINGO

OVAL   CIRCLE   RECTANGLE

12   © 2003 Jan Z. Olsen

GRAY

ELEPHANT   TRASH CAN   SCISSORS

OVAL   RECTANGLE   TRIANGLE

© 2003 Jan Z. Olsen   13

Pink

Ask about pink
Can you find the crayon? (Point)
This crayon is going to be pink.
Do you know anything that is pink?

Begin to look and learn
Let's find the pig. (Point)
Let's find the tutu. (Point)
Let's find the flamingo. (Point)
Let's find the oval. (Point)
Let's find the circle. (Point)
Let's find the rectangle. (Point)

Color
Color the pig, tutu, and flamingo pink.
Color the shapes below pink.

Demonstrate
Let's trace shapes. Put finger on shape and trace.

Extra
Point to pink items in the room.
Make pink by mixing red and white.
Stick out tongues. Notice they're pink.

Gray

Ask about gray
Can you find the crayon? (Point)
This crayon is going to be gray.
Do you know anything that is gray?

Begin to look and learn
Let's find the elephant. (Point)
Let's find the trash can. (Point)
Let's find the scissors. (Point)
Let's find the oval. (Point)
Let's find the rectangle. (Point)
Let's find the triangle. (Point)

Color
Color the elephant, trash can and scissors gray.
Color the shapes below gray.

Demonstrate
Let's trace shapes. Put finger on shape and trace.

Extra
Point to gray items in the room.
Make gray by mixing black and white.

Pictures, Colors, and Shapes, cont.

Coloring shapes naturally leads to other shape activities: counting sides and corners, folding squares to make triangles or rectangles, cutting and pasting shapes, and making shape designs and pictures. Read page 34 for more ideas.

Brown

Ask about brown
Can you find the crayon? (Point)
This crayon is going to be brown.
Do you know anything that is brown?

Begin to look and learn
Let's find the buffalo. (Point)
Let's find the bear. (Point)
Let's find the boot. (Point)
Let's find the rectangle. (Point)
Let's find the circle. (Point)
Let's find the triangle. (Point)

Color
Color the buffalo, bear and boot brown.
Color the shapes below brown.

Demonstrate
Let's trace shapes. Put finger on shape and trace.

Extra
Point to brown items in the room.
Mix red and green to make brown.

Black

Ask about black
Can you find the crayon? (Point)
This crayon is going to be black.
Do you know anything that is black?

Begin to look and learn
Let's find the crow. (Point)
Let's find the ink. (Point)
Let's find the licorice. (Point)
Let's find the oval. (Point)
Let's find the square. (Point)
Let's find the rectangle. (Point)

Color
Color the crow, ink and licorice black.
Color the shapes below black.
Let's sing the "Crayon Song."
Lyrics and activities for this song are on page 36.

Demonstrate
Let's trace shapes. Put finger on shape and trace.

Extra
Point to black items in the room.
See who's wearing black shoes.

48

Vertical and Horizontal

These pages give children experience with the simplest line to draw, the vertical line. The puffy fluffy activity teaches children how to make "rain" come down in the air with their hands, and then make little rain strokes down on paper.

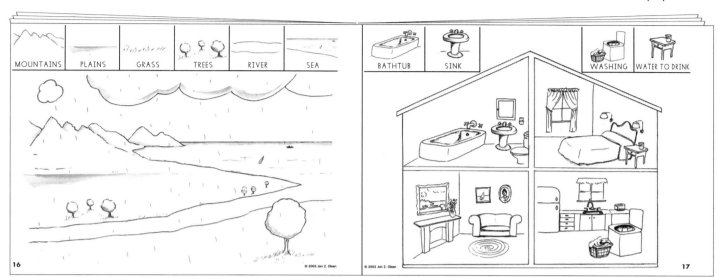

Talk about the page and the words in the song. Help children find the cloud, rain, mountains, etc. Explain that the plains are flat lands. Tell children that the page needs rain.
1. Pick up a blue crayon
2. Make "rain strokes" that fall down. (Demonstrate little "rain strokes" on paper.)

Use the house page as a discussion page. Talk about water in the bathtub and sink. Talk about water for washing and water to drink.
1. Pick up a blue crayon.
2. Color water for the bathtub, sink, washer and cup blue.
3. Make "rain strokes" and color the house.

Puffy Fluffy

Move to music. Make clouds and rain in the air.
Tune: Twinkle, Twinkle Little Star

I'm a cloud up in the sky, Puffy and fluffy and floating by
When I'm full of water, I rain
Down on the mountains, Down on the plains
Rain for the grass, Rain for the trees
Rain for the rivers and the big blue seas

I'm a cloud up in the sky, Puffy and fluffy and floating by
When I'm full of water I rain
Down on the mountains, Down on the plains
Water for the bathtub, Water for the sink
Water for washing and water to drink

I'm a cloud up in the sky, Puffy and fluffy and floating by
When I'm full of water, I rain
Down on the mountains, Down on the plains
I'm a cloud up in the sky, Look up at me I'm floating by

Suggested Activities
- Use large movements with the song. Put hands above head like a cloud (make a circle with arms). Use fingers to represent the rain coming down.

Vertical and Horizontal, cont.

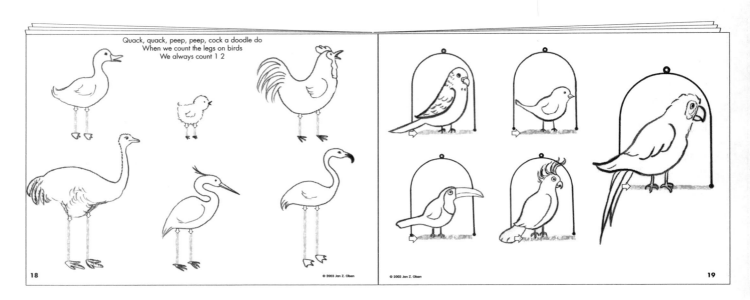

Quack, quack, peep, peep, cock a doodle do
When we count the legs on birds
We always count 1 2

18   © 2003 Jan Z. Olsen   © 2003 Jan Z. Olsen   19

Birds

Vertical ↓ down strokes are developmentally the easiest strokes to learn.

Ask about legs and birds
How many legs do you have?
How many legs do birds have?
Are the birds standing or flying?

Begin to look and learn
The page has a duck, chick and rooster.
The ostrich, heron, and flamingo may be new.
Show pictures.
Talk about size, color, and bird behavior.

Color and draw
Color the birds.

Demonstrate tracing down ↓
Let's trace the legs.
Put the crayon on the ⇩.
Go down. Stop at the feet.

Extra
Play and learn the "Bird Legs" chant. It is track #12 on the CD and there are activities for this song on page 88.

Horizontal → strokes are the next strokes children learn.

Ask about perches and birds
Does anyone have a pet bird?
Does it look like one of these?
Where do birds like to stand/perch?
Has a bird ever perched on your finger?

Begin to look and learn
Are the birds the same or different?
Which one is the biggest?

Color and draw
The birds are a parakeet, canary, toucan, cockatoo, and parrot.
Show pictures and help children choose colors for the birds.

Demonstrate tracing across →
Let's make perches for the birds.
Put the crayon on the ⇨.
Go across.

Extra
Ask if anyone has a pet bird they can bring to show.

Teacher's Guide, p. 88

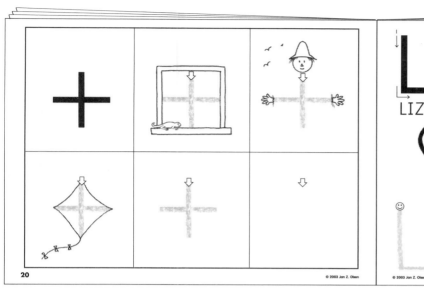

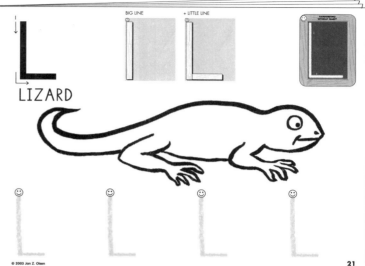

LIZARD

Teaching Cross + and L

Preparation for +
Prepare children for L by drawing a cross. Developmentally, the cross is taught after circle. However, because we are teaching a letter with horizontal/vertical strokes, we teach cross now. Demonstrate cross for students. Have students put their crayons on the arrow. Say "Big line down, big line across. Look, we made a cross." Allow children to choose which picture they would like to turn their final shape into. Children who are not ready for crayon tracing can finger trace over each cross. It's fine if a child doesn't cross exactly in the middle. Have students look for the lizard on the cross page.

Ask about L
Do you know: L words? L names? L sounds?
Have you ever seen a lizard?

Begin to look and learn
This is the L page. Let's find L's on this page. (Point)
Look. There's a lizard. (Point)
Lizard starts with L.
Is a lizard an animal or a person? Where do lizards live?
What do lizards have? What color/s are lizards? (Show pictures.)

Color and draw
Let's color the lizard. (Show different ways to color.)
What about adding spots or stripes? Rocks or grass for the lizard? (Demonstrate.)
The lizard needs a tongue!

Demonstrate tracing L
Let's write L for lizard. Put the crayon on the ☺.
Big line down. Little line across.

Extra
Stick tongue out like a lizard. Move it up and down and side–to–side.

Fun Focus
Talk about in and out. Is the lizard's tongue in or out?

Note: Make up verses for "cross" like those on track 17.

Teacher's Guide, p. 90

Vertical and Horizontal, cont.

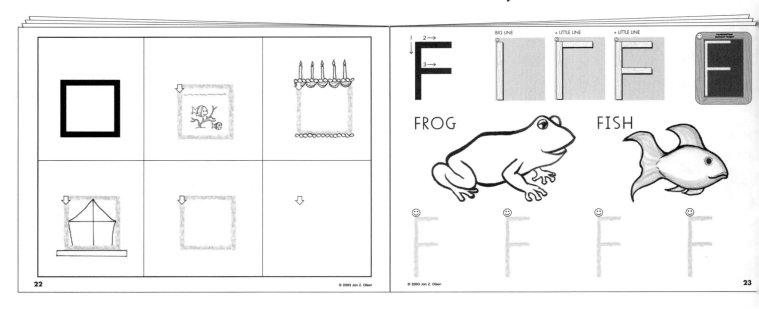

Teaching Square □ and F

Preparation for Square □
Developmentally, the square is taught after the cross. This shape contains vertical and horizontal strokes. Demonstrate square for the students. Have students put their crayons on the arrow. Say "big line down, big line across the bottom, big line up, big line across the top. Look, we made a square." Use "My Teacher Draws," track #17, on the Sing Along CD to teach simple shape drawing. (See page 90.) Allow children to choose which picture they would like to turn their final shape into. Children who are not ready for crayon tracing can finger trace over each square. Have students look for the fish on the square page.

Ask about F
Do you know: F words? F names? F sounds? F months?
Have you seen a frog or a fish?

Begin to look and learn
This is the F page. Let's find the F's. (Point)
Look. There's a frog and a fish. (Point)
Frog and fish start with F.
Talk about: how they move, where they live, 4 legs and no legs, 1 tail, fins.

Color and draw
Color the frog and fish. (Show different ways to color.)
What about adding water and grass?

Demonstrate tracing F
Let's write F. Put the crayon on the ☺.
Big line down. Jump to the ☺. Little line across the top.
Little line across the middle.

Extra
Cup one hand. Hold the other hand in a fist and pretend it's a frog jumping on the other hand. Jump like a frog with large movements around the classroom.

Fun Focus
Swim around room like a fish. Jump like a frog.

Teacher's Guide, p. 90

Vertical and Horizontal, cont.

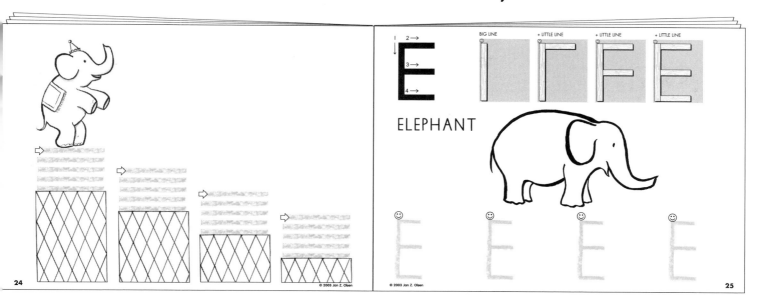

ELEPHANT

Teaching E

Pre-Stroke for E
Prepare children for E with this pre-stroke page. This page has horizontal lines for tracing. Developmentally, the horizontal line is taught after the vertical line and is one of the easiest strokes for a child. Demonstrate horizontal lines for students. Have them put their crayons on the arrow. Say "big line across. Stop. Look, we made a line." Children who are not ready for crayon tracing can finger trace over each line. It's fine if a child makes the line a little too long. With practice, they will learn to stop with more control. Color the page.

Ask about E
Do you know: E words? E names? E sounds?
Have you seen an elephant?

Begin to look and learn
This is the E page. Let's find the E's. (Point)
Look. There's an elephant. (Point)
Elephant starts with E.
Talk about: body parts, nose/trunk and how it's used, big ears,
4 legs 1 tail; elephant size, sound, where elephants live.

Color and draw
Remind children about using a good crayon grip by singing the "Crayon Song,"
track #5 on the Sing Along CD.
Color elephant gray.
What about adding peanuts, trees and grass?

Demonstrate tracing E
Let's write E. Put the crayon on the ☺.
Big line down. Jump to the ☺. Little line across the top, middle, and bottom.

Extra
Bend over, put hands together, use arms as a trunk and swing side to side.

Fun Focus
Compare heavy and light.

Vertical and Horizontal, cont.

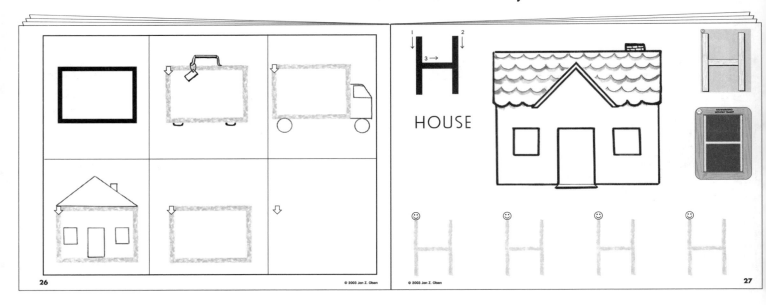

Teaching Rectangle ▭ and H

Preparation for ▭
Rectangles use vertical and horizontal lines. Demonstrate rectangle for the students. Have them put their crayons on the arrow. Say, "little line down, big line across the bottom, little line up, big line across the top. Look, we made a rectangle." Allow children to choose which picture they would like to turn their final shape into. Children who are not ready for crayon tracing may finger trace over each rectangle. Have students look for the house on the rectangle page.

Ask about H
Do you know: H words? H names? H sounds?
Have you seen a house? Who lives in a house? Does your house have a chimney?
What does the chimney do?

Begin to look and learn
This is the H page. Let's find the H's. (Point)
Look. There's a house. (Point)
House starts with H.
Talk about: 1 house, 1 door, 1 chimney, 2 windows.

Color and draw
Sing the "Crayon Song" (see page 36). Color house any color.
What about adding grass, doorknob, smoke from chimney, window panes?

Demonstrate tracing H
Let's trace H. Put the crayon on the ☺.
Big line down. Big line down. Little line across.

Extra
Tell the story of the 3 Little Pigs.

Fun Focus
Make a house out of a cardboard box.

Teacher's Guide, p. 90

54

Note: Make up verses for "rectangle" like those on track 17.

Vertical and Horizontal, cont.

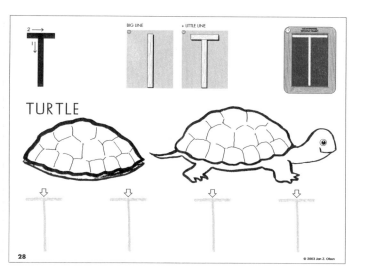

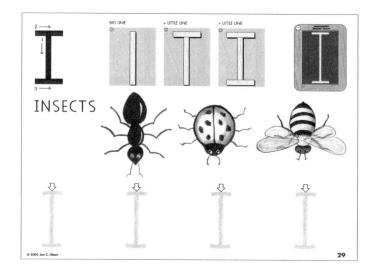

Teaching T

Ask about T
Do you know: T words? T names? T sounds? T days?
Have you seen a turtle?

Begin to look and learn
This is the T page. Let's find the T's. (Point)
Look. There's a turtle. (Point)
Turtle starts with T.
Talk about: opposites in/out, hard/soft, where turtles live, 4 legs, how turtles hide in the shell, swim in water.

Color and draw
Sing the "Crayon Song" (see page 36).
Color the turtle brown or green.
What about adding water, a sun, rocks?

Demonstrate tracing T
Let's write T. Put the crayon on the ⬇.
Big line down.
Little line across top.

Extra
Make turtles as a craft project.

Fun Focus
Make T for Time Out with your arms, just like a referee.

Teaching I

Ask about I
Do you know: I words? I names? I sounds?
Have you seen insects?

Begin to look and learn
This is the I page. Let's find the I's. (Point)
Look. There are insects. (Point)
Insects start with I.
Talk about: where insects live, 6 legs, 2 antenna, wings to fly, another name for insects, size.

Color and draw
Color the ladybug red and bee yellow.
What about drawing another insect or bug?

Demonstrate tracing I
Let's write I. Put the crayon on the ⬇.
Big line down.
Little line across the top and little line across the bottom.

Extra
Fly around like insects.
Sing, "The Ant, The Bug and The Bee" song, track #14.

Teacher's Guide, p. 43

Vertical and Horizontal, cont.

Teaching Rain Song Page

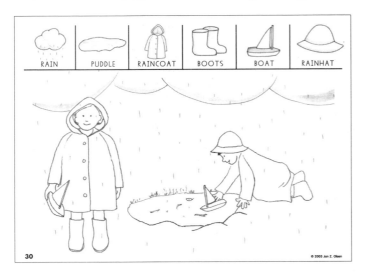

30
© 2003 Jan Z. Olsen

This is a page for coloring! The page goes along with the "Rain Song" (track #24) on the Sing Along CD. Children enjoy finding the pictures at the top in the big picture below.

Rain Song

It's raining, it's pouring
Puddles in the street
I've got my raincoat
Boots for my feet

I'm going outside
Playing with Sam
We'll find a puddle and
We'll make a dam
It's raining, it's pouring
Let's get a boat

It's raining, it's pouring
Little sticks will float
It's raining, it's pouring
Such a happy day

I love when it rains
And we go out to play

Teaching U

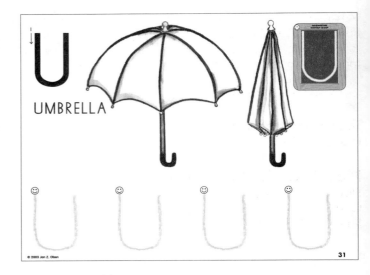

© 2003 Jan Z. Olsen
31

Ask about U
Do you know: U words? U names? U sounds?
Have you used an umbrella?

Begin to look and learn
This is the U page. Let's find the U's. (Point)
Look. There's an umbrella. (Point)
Umbrella starts with U.
Talk about opposites: open/shut, up/down, wet/dry.

Color and draw
Color the umbrella. What about using different colors for each section of the umbrella?

Demonstrate tracing U
Let's trace U. Put the crayon on the ☺.
Big line down. Turn and go across the bottom.
Big line up.

Extra
Make an umbrella, raincoat and boots for Mat Man™.

Fun Focus
Use toy cars and make U turns.

Suggested Activities
- Color the page while the CD is playing the song.
- On a rainy day, give Mat Man™ boots too. Discuss what to wear on a rainy day.
- Test objects for sinking and floating. Try little sticks and boats.

56

© 2005 Jan Z. Olsen

Magic C

Meet the Magic C Bunny!

Making C strokes prepares children for drawing circles and writing. Children may have made circular scribbles by starting anywhere and just going round and round. Now it's time for the teacher, the Magic C Bunny and the "Magic C" song (page 86) to teach them how to start:

- Circles
- Letters—C O Q G S

This habit is important now and will be even more important in kindergarten when they learn the lower case letters that start with a Magic c stroke, a, d, g, o and q.

I'm the Magic C Bunny!

Play Magic C Bunny Says....

Play Simon Says as Magic C Bunny Says. Have the puppet whisper in your ear when you say "Magic C Bunny Says." Other times, just give the direction without the puppet whispering in your ear and without saying "Magic C Bunny Says." Children should only follow when you say "Magic C Bunny Says."

Making Your Own Magic C Bunnies

You may purchase a Magic C Bunny from HWT. Here's how to make one from a napkin.

1

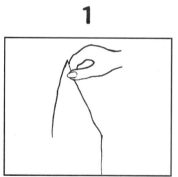

Open a paper napkin. Hold by one corner.

2

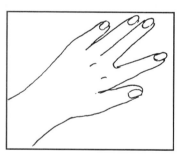

Spread index and middle fingers apart.

3

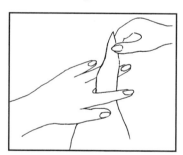

Pull corner between your index and middle fingers. (First ear)

4

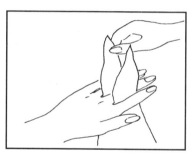

Take the next corner. Pull corner between your middle and ring fingers. (Second ear)

5

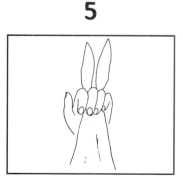

Fold fingers into palm.

6

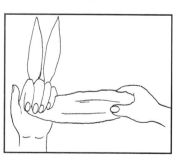

Pull napkin out to side.

7

Wrap napkin over fingers and tuck into hand.

8

Add the face with a pen. It's a bunny! You may slip the bunny off your fingers and give it to a child. Tape or staple the napkin to hold it.

Magic C, cont.

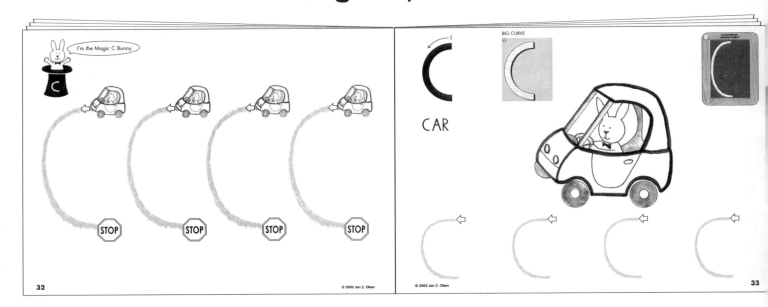

Teaching C

Pre-stroke for C
Prepare children for C with this pre-stroke page. Use the Magic C Bunny puppet to help you teach. Demonstrate Magic C's for students. Have them put their crayons on the arrow. Say "Magic C Bunny wants us to make a Magic C to help get his car to the stop sign. Magic C. Stop. Look, we made a Magic C." Make car sounds while tracing the stroke. Use the HWT Sing Along CD (track #6) to teach "Magic C" (see page 86). Children who are not ready for crayon tracing can finger trace over each Magic C. Color the page.

Ask about C
Do you know...any words that start with C? any names that start with C? the C sound?
Have you ever seen a car like this one?

Begin to look and learn
This is the C page. Let's find C's on this page. (Point)
Look. There's a car. (Point)
Car starts with C.
Is a car alive? Is it an animal, a person or a thing? What do cars do? What do cars have?
What color cars have you seen? (Show pictures.)

Color and draw
Let's color the car. (Show different ways to color.)
Any designs? Does your car need a road? (Demonstrate.)

Demonstrate tracing C
Let's write C for car. Put the crayon on the ⬅.
Big curve. Stop at the bottom.
Sing the "Magic C" song, track #6 on the Sing Along CD.

Teacher's Guide, p. 86

Extra
Curve left hand to make C. Use right index finger to trace C.

Fun Focus
Use the Magic C Bunny puppet to introduce C or make your own (see previous page).

Note: *Get Set for School*™ uses pictures and ☺ or ⬆ icons to help children start shapes and letters correctly.

Magic C, cont.

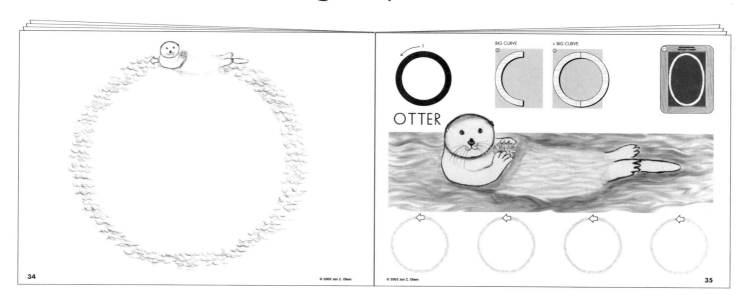

Teaching O

Pre-stroke for O
Prepare children for O with this pre-stroke page. This page has water in the shape of an O for tracing. Demonstrate the O stroke for students. Have students put their crayons on the arrow. Say, "Magic C. Keep going. Stop at the top. Look we traced an O." Children who are not yet ready for crayon tracing can finger trace around the circle of water. Encourage the child to go around more than once. Color the page.

Ask about O
Do you know: O words? O names? O months? O sounds?
Have you seen an otter?

Begin to look and learn
This is the O page. Let's find the O's. (Point)
Look. There's an otter. (Point)
Otter starts with O.
Talk about: where the otter lives, what he's doing,
shape of head, floating on back.

Color and draw
Color the otter and the water.

Demonstrate tracing O
Let's write O. Put the crayon on the ⇦ .
Magic C. Keep going. Stop at the top.

Extra
Have Cheerios® or round pretzels for a snack.

Fun Focus
Make Os with wood pieces first. See page 12.

Magic C, cont.

Teaching Circle ◯ and Q

Preparation for ◯

Prepare children for Q by drawing a circle. Developmentally, the circle is taught after the horizontal line. Demonstrate circle for the students. Have them put their crayons on the arrow. Say "Magic C. Keep going. Look we made a circle." Use the HWT Sing Along CD (track #6 or #17) to teach simple drawings using circle. Allow children to choose which picture they would like to turn their final shape into. Children who are not ready for crayon tracing can finger trace over each circle.

Ask about Q

Do you know: Q words? Q names? Q sounds?
Have you seen a quilt?

Begin to look and learn

This is the Q page. Let's find the Q's. (Point)
Look. There's a quilt. (Point)
Quilt starts with Q.
Talk about how quilts: keep us warm, are made of pieces, have lots of colors.

Color and draw

Color the quilt. Use many colors to aim and scribble on the squares.

Demonstrate tracing Q

Let's write Q. Put the crayon on the ⬅.
Magic C. Keep going. Stop at the top. Add a little line.

Extra

Do this Q activity. Act like ducks and say QUACK, QUACK, QUACK. Then say QUIET and stop. Repeat.

Fun Focus

Bring in quilts or blankets. Have children get "under" a quilt and be quiet.

Teacher's Guide, p. 90

Magic C, cont.

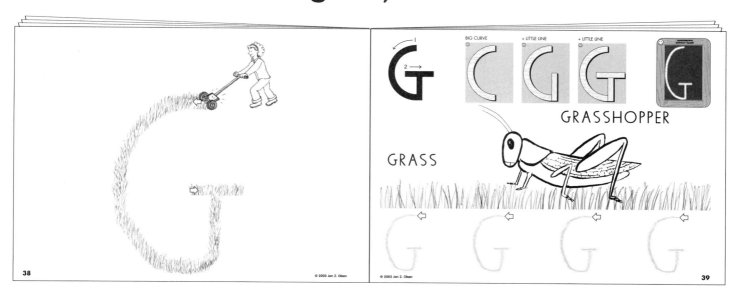

GRASS

GRASSHOPPER

BIG CURVE + LITTLE LINE + LITTLE LINE

38 © 2003 Jan Z. Olsen © 2003 Jan Z. Olsen 39

Teaching G

Pre-Stroke for G
Get ready for G by cutting the grass. Demonstrate the formation of G. Have students put their crayons on the arrow. Say, "Magic C, little line up, little line across. Look, we traced G." Make mowing sounds as you trace. Children who are not ready for crayon tracing can finger trace. Color the page.

Ask about G
Do you know: G words? G names? G sounds?
(Note: G sounds like J in George/gym/gentle.)
Have you seen a grasshopper?

Begin to look and learn
This is the G Page. Let's find the G's. (Point)
Look. There's a grasshopper in the grass. (Point)
They start with G.
Talk about: insects, 6 legs with 2 big ones for hopping, cutting grass.

Color and draw
Color using two shades of green.
What about adding a bug or a worm in the grass?

Demonstrate tracing G
Let's write G. Put the crayon on the ⟵.
Magic C. Little line up. Little line across.

Extra
Hop like grasshoppers. Make cuts on green paper to make grass.

Fun Focus
Wear green. Eat green snacks.

Magic C, cont.

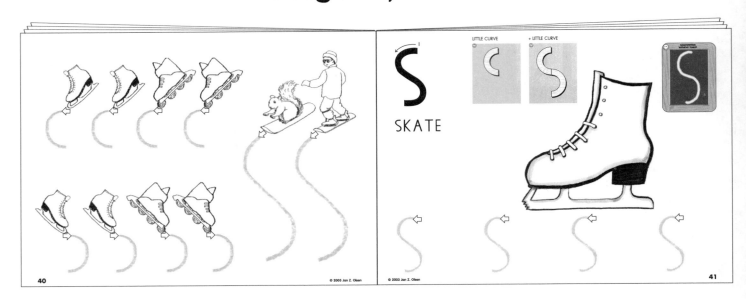

Teaching S

Pre-Stroke for S
Prepare children for S with this pre-stroke page. This page has little curves and curves in the shape of an S for tracing. Demonstrate little curves. Have students put their crayons on the arrow. Say "Little curve. Stop. Look, we made a little curve." Demonstrate skating the other way. Now make the skateboarding squirrel and child ride down with an S curve. Children who are not ready for crayon tracing can finger trace over the curves. It's fine if a child does not stop exactly at the end of the stroke. With practice, they will learn to stop. Color the page.

Ask about S
Do you know: S words? S names? S sounds? S days? S month?
Have you seen a skate?

Begin to look and learn
This is the S page. Let's find the S's. (Point)
Look. There's a skate. (Point)
Skate starts with S.
Talk about: places you can skate, who has skates, if they have seen anyone skate.

Color and draw
Color the skate.

Demonstrate tracing S
Let's write S. Put the crayon on the ⬅.
Make a little Magic c curve. Make a little curve the other way.

Extra
Children can make a snake into an S.

Fun Focus
Children can pretend that they are skating around the room.

Teaching J

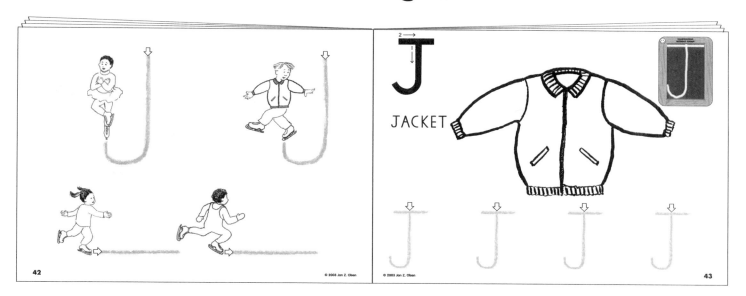

Pre-Stroke for J

Prepare for J by pretend skating. Demonstrate the J turn for students. Say, "Big line down. Turn. Stop." Demonstrate little lines. Have students put their crayons on the arrow. Say "Little line across. Stop." Children who are not ready for crayon tracing can finger trace. It's fine if a child makes the line a little too long at first. With practice, they will learn to stop. Color the page.

Ask about J

Do you know: J words? J names? J sounds? J months?
Do you have a jacket?

Begin to look and learn

This is the J page. Let's find the J's. (Point)
Look. There's a jacket. (Point)
Jacket starts with J.
Talk about: January and June weather, hanging up jackets,
parts of a jacket, how many sleeves?

Color and draw

Color the jacket.

Demonstrate tracing J

Let's write J. Put the crayon on the ⇩.
Big line down. Turn. Little line across the top.

Extra

J is for jumping too. Jump around the room.
J is for jogging. Jog around the room.

Fun Focus

Practice putting on and taking off jackets. Practice zipping or buttoning.
Teach up/down, on/off and open/closed concepts. Make a jacket for Mat Man™.

Big and Little Curves

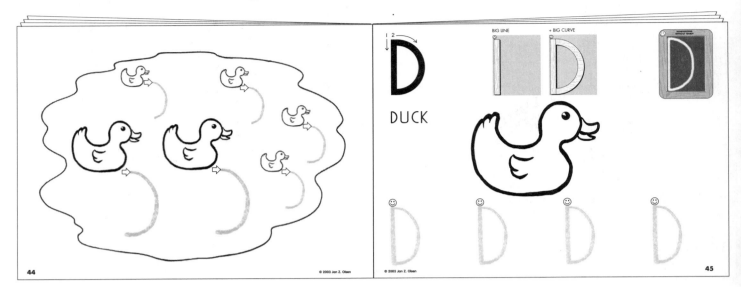

Teaching D

Pre-Stroke for D

Prepare children for D, P, B and R with this pre-stroke page. Demonstrate big curves using the big ducks. Have them put their crayons on the arrow. Say "Big curve. Stop. Look, we made a big curve." Teach little curves with the little ducks. Quack like ducks as you're making the strokes. Children who are not ready for crayon tracing can finger trace. Initially, it's fine if a child doesn't stop at the end of the curve. With practice, they will learn to stop. Color the page.

Ask about D

Do you know: D words? D months? D names? D sounds?
Have you ever seen a duck?

Begin to look and learn

This is the D page. Let's find D's on this page. (Point)
Look. There's a duck. (Point)
Duck starts with D.
Is a duck an animal or a person?
Where do ducks live? What do ducks have? What color/s are ducks? (Show pictures.)

Color and draw

Let's color the duck. (Show different ways to color.)

Demonstrate tracing D

Let's write D.
Put the crayon on the ☺.
Big line down. Jump back to ☺. Big curve to the bottom.

Extra

Make duck sounds. Fly or walk like ducks.

Fun Focus

Float a rubber ducky. Play with sinking and floating things.

Big and Little Curves, cont.

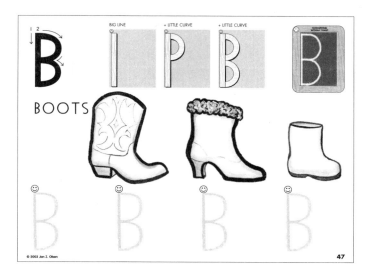

Teaching P

Ask about P
Do you know: P words? P names? P sounds?
Have you seen a pail?

Begin to look and learn
This is the P page. Let's find the P's. (Point)
Look. There's a pail. (Point)
Pail starts with P.
Talk about: how pails are used, what goes in them,
Jack and Jill Nursery Rhyme.

Color and draw
Color the pail. What about putting something in it?

Demonstrate tracing P
Let's write P. Put the crayon on the ☺.
Big line down. Jump to the ☺.
Little curve to the middle.

Extra
Make a bucket brigade and pass the pail like firefighters
did long ago.

Fun Focus
Teach in/out by placing things in pails.
P is for Peppermint. Smell peppermint.

Teaching B

Ask about B
Do you know: B words? B names? B sounds?
Do you have boots?

Begin to look and learn
This is the B page. Let's find the B's. (Point)
Look. There are three boots. (Point)
Boot starts with B.
Talk about: different purpose boots, baby booties,
big/little boots

Color and draw
Color the boots any color.
What about adding mud, puddle, grass? (Demonstrate.)

Demonstrate tracing B
Let's write B. Put the crayon on the ☺.
Big line down. Jump to the ☺.
Little curve to the middle. Little curve to the bottom.

Extra
B is for ball.
Sort balls by color, type and size.

Fun Focus
Talk about cowboy boots and pretend to ride horses.

Diagonals

Teaching R

Pre-Stroke for R
Prepare children for the diagonal in R with this pre-stroke page. Diagonal lines are the most difficult. Have students put their crayons on the arrow. Say, "Slide down the rake handle. Stop." Children who are not ready for crayon tracing can finger trace over each line. Color the page. Add leaves on the ground.

Ask about R
Do you know: R words? R names? R sounds?
Have you seen a rake?
Have you ever used a rake?
What do rakes do?

Begin to look and learn
This is the R page. Let's find the R's. (Point)
Look. There's a rake. (Point)
Rake starts with R.
Talk about: 1 handle.

Color and draw
Color rake any color.
What about adding leaves, grass? (Demonstrate.)

Demonstrate tracing R
Let's trace R. Put the crayon on the ☺.
Big line down. Jump to the ☺. Little curve to the middle.
Little line to the corner.

Extra
Rake leaves. Use a rake to make patterns in a sandbox. R is for run. Go outside and run.

Fun Focus
Find everything that is red in the room. Who's wearing red?

66

Diagonals, cont.

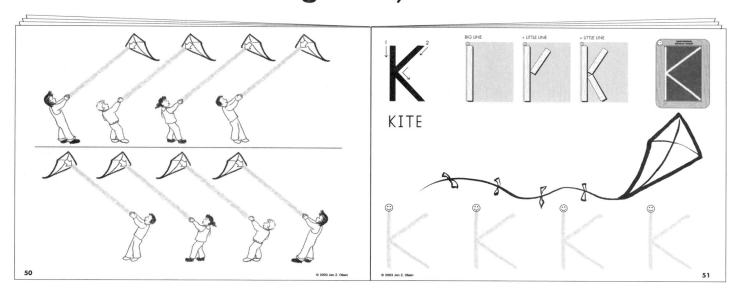

Teaching K

Pre-Stroke for K
Prepare children for K with this pre-stroke page. This page has little diagonal lines for tracing. Because the stroke begins at the kite and ends at the child's hand, this gives children practice with the ability to start/stop. Have students put their crayons on the arrow. Say "Slide down the kite string to the hands." Make noises like the wind as you're making the strokes. Children who are not ready for crayon tracing can finger trace over each line. Color the page. Use different color crayons.

Ask about K
Do you know: K words? K names? K sounds?
Have you flown a kite?

Begin to look and learn
This is the K page. Let's find the K's. (Point)
Look. There' a kite. (Point)
Kite starts with K.
Talk about: wind, different types of kites.

Color and draw
Color the kites any color.

Demonstrate tracing K
Let's write K. Put the crayon on the ☺.
Big line down. Jump to the other corner.
Little line slides to the middle, little line slides to the bottom.

Extra
Make kites. Wind string.

Fun Focus
Pretend to give the K a Karate Kick when making the letter.

Diagonals, cont.

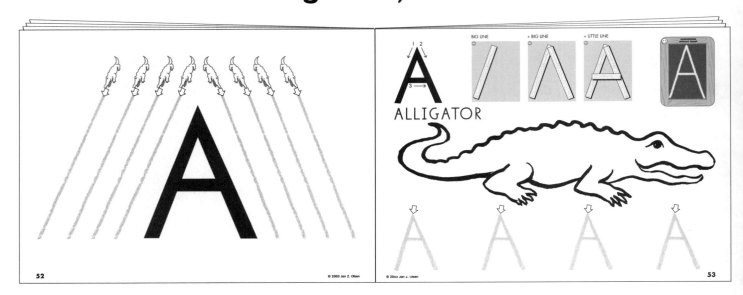

Teaching A

Pre-Stroke for A
The first letter of the alphabet is one of the most difficult. A frequent mistake children make is starting at the bottom. That's why the pre-stroke page is so important. Demonstrate starting at the top where the alligators are. Put the crayon on the arrow, say, "Big line slides down. Stop." Make noises like the alligator is eating the crayon stroke "chomp, chomp, chomp" as you're making the strokes. Children who are not ready for crayon tracing can finger trace over each line. Color the alligators. Use different crayons to make each stroke. This also gives practice with picking up and holding a crayon correctly.

Ask about A
Do you know: A words? A names? A sounds? A months?
Have you seen an alligator?

Begin to look and learn
This is the A page. Let's find the A's. (Point)
Look. There's an alligator. (Point)
Alligator starts with A.
Talk about: where alligators live, 1 tail, lots of teeth, 4 legs.

Color and draw
Color the alligator green.
What about adding water, a sun, rocks. (Demonstrate.)

Demonstrate tracing A
Let's write A. Put the crayon on the ⬦.
Big line slides down. Jump back to the top.
Big line slides down. Little line across.

Extra
Crawl on the floor like alligators. Make hand shadow alligator mouths.

Fun Focus
A is for apple. Sort apples by color and size.

Diagonals, cont.

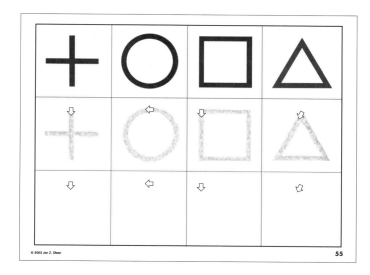

Teaching Triangle

Developmentally, the triangle comes after the square. Demonstrate triangle for students. Have students put their crayons on the ⬨. Say "big line down, big line across the bottom, big line back to the ⬨. Look, we made a triangle." Use the "My Teacher Draws" song, track #17, from the Sing Along CD (See page 90 for lyrics and activities with this song.) Allow children to choose which picture they would like to turn their final shape into. Children who are not ready for crayon tracing can finger trace over each triangle. It's fine if a child makes a triangle that isn't identical to the one used in the book. There are different triangles.

Teaching Shape Review

On the first row, have the child tell you the name of the first shape. Below, have the child trace the first shape. If the child can trace the shape, then try copying the shape directly below the traced shape. Repeat until all shapes are complete or until the child indicates they are at a level of completion.

Teacher's Guide, p. 90

Diagonals, cont.

Teaching V

Pre-Stroke for V
Prepare children for V and W with this pre-stroke page. This page has a roller coaster in the shape of a V. Demonstrate big line slides down, big line slides up. Have students put their crayons on the arrow. Say "Big line slides down, big line slides up. Look, we moved like a V." Allow children to make noises as if they are on a roller coaster while making the strokes. Color the page.

Ask about V
Do you know: V words? V names? V sounds?
Have you been in a van?

Begin to look and learn
This is the V page. Let's find V's on this page. (Point)
Look. There's a van. (Point)
Van starts with V.
What do vans do?
What color/s are vans? (Show pictures.)

Color and draw
Let's color the van. (Show different ways to color.)
Draw people in the van.

Demonstrate tracing V
Let's write V for van.
Put the crayon on the ☺.
Big line slides down. Big line slides up.

Extra
Make fingers into Vs.

Fun Focus
Make V with wood pieces.

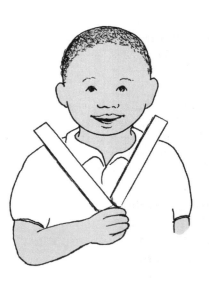

70

Diagonals, cont.

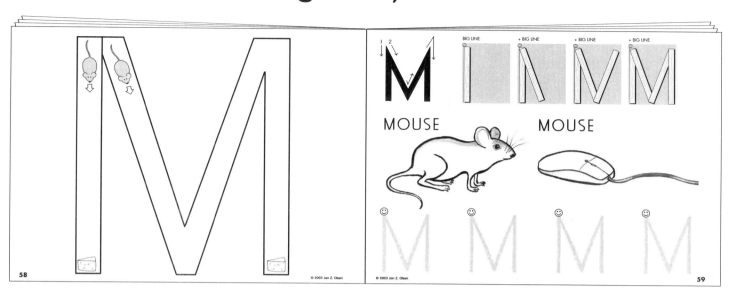

Teaching M

Pre-Stroke for M

Prepare children for M with this pre-stroke page. The mice are looking for cheese. Demonstrate big line down. Have students put their crayons on the arrow by the first mouse. Say "Big line down. Stop. Now put the crayon on the next arrow. Big line slides down, big line slides up, big line down. Look, it looks like M." Make "sniffing" sounds while making the strokes. Encourage children to trace more than once with different colors. By using more than one color, children get practice picking up and holding their crayons.

Ask about M

Do you know: M words? M names? M sounds? M months? M day?
Have you seen a mouse?

Begin to look and learn

This is the M page. Let's find the M's. (Point)
Look. There's a mouse. Look, there's a different mouse (a computer mouse). (Point)
Mouse starts with M.
Talk about mice: their size, where they live, what they eat.

Color and draw

Color both mice. What about adding cheese?

Demonstrate tracing M

Let's trace M. Put the crayon on the ☺.
Big line down. Jump to the ☺. Big line slides down. And up. And down.

Extra

Three Blind Mice Nursery Rhyme.

Fun Focus

M is for Middle. Play with Mat Man™ and put a belly button in the middle of his body.

Diagonals, cont.

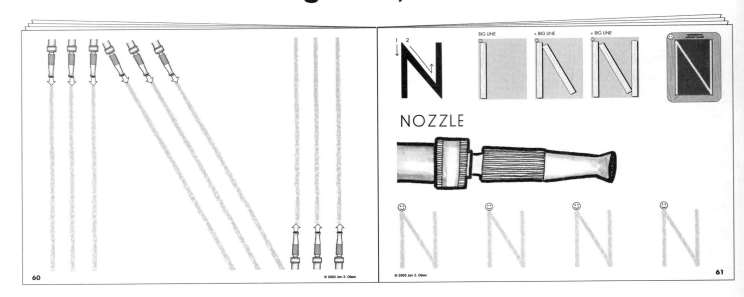

Teaching N

Pre-Stroke for N
Prepare children for N with this pre-stroke page. This page has nozzles squirting water vertically and diagonally. Demonstrate big lines down, big lines diagonally, and big lines up. Have students put their crayons on the arrow. Say "Big line down, big line slides down, big line up. Look, we moved like an N." Use a blue crayon for water. Color the nozzles.

Ask about N
Do you know: N words? N names? N sounds?
Have you seen squirted water with a nozzle?

Begin to look and learn
This is the N page. Let's find the N's. (Point)
Look. There's a nozzle (Point)
Nozzle starts with N.
Talk about: what nozzles do, what comes out of a nozzle, on/off concepts, what you can water.

Color and draw
Color the nozzle. Draw water squirting out of the nozzle.

Demonstrate tracing N
Let's write N. Put the crayon on the ☺.
Big line down. Jump to the ☺. Big line slides down. Big line goes up.

Extra
N is for no. Shake head for no. Nod head for yes.
Play with hose and nozzle. Squirt water.

Fun Focus
N is for noise. Make car, truck, and airplane noises.

Diagonals, cont.

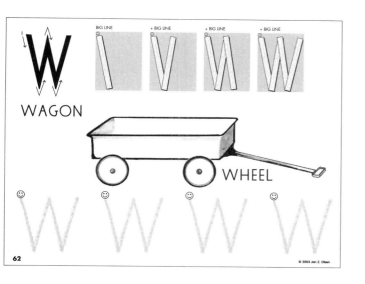

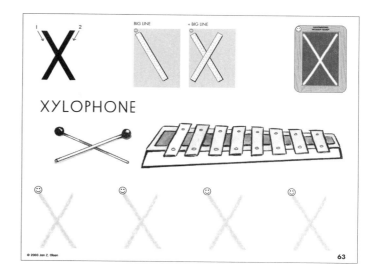

Teaching W

Ask about W
Do you know: W words? W names? W sounds? W day? Have you seen a wagon?

Begin to look and learn
This is the W page. Let's find the W's. (Point)
Look. There's an a wagon and a wheel (Point)
Wagon and wheel start with W.
Talk about: opposites (in/out, push/pull, on/off, empty/full) riding in a wagon, how wheels work.

Color and draw
Color wagon red and wheels black.
What about adding grass, rocks, dirt, or a person riding in the wagon?

Demonstrate tracing W
Let's trace W. Put the crayon on the ☺.
Big line slides down. And up. And down. And up.

Extra
Make covered wagons out of cardboard boxes.
Count wheels on bikes, tricycles and cars.
Make cars slide down ramps.

Fun Focus
W is for white and winter. Use a Q–Tip to dab white snow spots on blue paper.

Teaching X

Ask about X
Do you know: X words? X names? X sounds?
Have you seen a xylophone?

Begin to look and learn
This is the X page. Let's find the X's. (Point)
Look. There's a xylophone (Point)
Xylophone starts with X, but it doesn't make an X sound.
Talk about: what a xylophone is, how they are played.

Color and draw
Color xylophone.

Demonstrate tracing X
Let's write X. Put the crayon on the ☺.
Big line down. Jump to the top of the other big line.
Big line down.

Extra
Play a xylophone. Make X with two big lines.

Fun Focus
Find EXIT signs. Play trains. Make a railroad crossing sign.

Diagonals, cont.

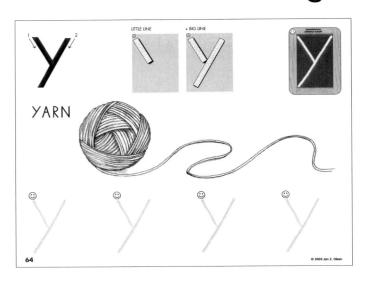

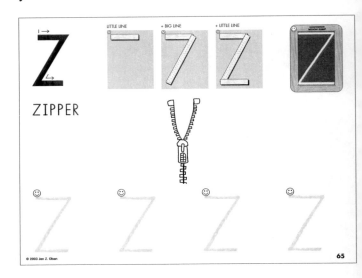

Teaching Y

Ask about Y
Do you know: Y words? Y names? Y sounds?
Have you seen yarn?

Begin to look and learn
This is the Y page. Let's find the Y's. (Point)
Look. There's yarn. (Point)
Yarn starts with Y.
Talk about: the shape (round), what it's used for,
color, long/short.

Color and draw
Color the yarn yellow.

Demonstrate tracing Y
Let's trace Y. Put the crayon on the ☺.
Little line slides down to the middle.
Jump to the top of the big line. Big line slides down.

Extra
Snip pieces of yarn. Make Y with yarn.
Glue yarn on a Y card.

Fun Focus
Find everything that's yellow in the room. See who's
wearing yellow.

Teaching Z

Ask about Z
Do you know: Z words? Z names? Z sounds?
Do you have a zipper on your clothes?

Begin to look and learn
This is the Z page. Let's find the Z's. (Point)
Look. There's a zipper. (Point)
Zipper start with Z.
Talk about: zippers on clothes, zip lock bags.

Color and draw
Color the zipper gray or silver.

Demonstrate tracing Z
Let's trace Z. Put the crayon on the ☺.
Little line across the top. Big line slides down.
Little line across.

Extra
Bring in purses and small cases to zip and unzip.

Fun Focus
Sing a zoo animals version of the "Animal Legs" song,
track #13. Include a zebra.
Make 2 big curves into a huge zero and say zero.
See page 12.

Diagonals, cont.

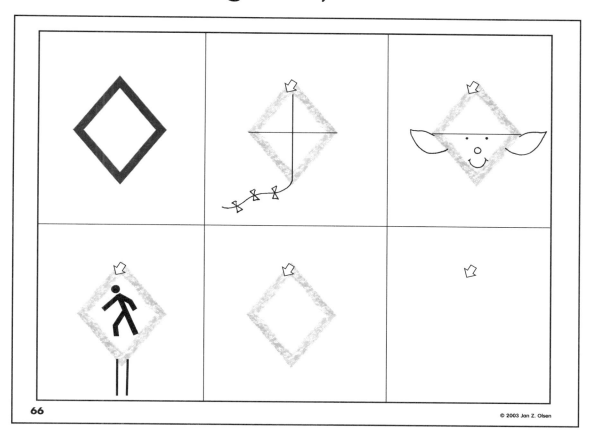

66

Teaching Diamond Page

The diamond shape is the most difficult shape. Demonstrate diamond for students. Have students put their crayons on the arrow. Say "Little line slides down, little line slides down, little line slides up, little line slides up. Look, we made a diamond." Allow children to choose which picture they would like to turn their final shape into. Children who are not ready for crayon tracing can finger trace over each diamond.

Teacher's Guide, p. 90

Numbers

From the time children first hold up their fingers to show how old they are, numbers are an important part of life. The program teaches numbers naturally through body awareness. Finger–plays and songs such as "Mat Man™," "Count On Me," "Five Fingers Play" and "Toe Song" give a physical understanding of numbers.

It's fun to learn numbers with songs about animals. Children sing, but they also move, touch, handle, and look as part of the song activity. For example: Children sing the "Animal Legs" song, track #13, pick up a toy animal and count the legs. "2 legs in the front, 2 legs in the back, the horse has 4 legs!" This guide also has suggestions for using objects to teach numbers.

Children learn number symbols 1 2 3 4 5 by placing wood pieces on the mat and by using the HWT slate chalkboard. See the "Wet–Dry–Try" method on the opposite page. In the workbook, children point, count and color. They learn to crayon trace just 1 2 3 4 5, but they learn to count and recognize numbers 6 7 8 9 10.

Your children will learn to:
1. **Count out loud**—Children say the numbers one through ten in order.
2. **Count with meaning**—Children learn how many for numbers one through ten. They count on themselves, animals and objects. They learn to touch and count.
3. **Build, Recognize and Trace Numbers**—Children become familiar with number symbols by using wood pieces, the "Wet–Dry–Try" slate activity and workbook lessons.

Teaching *Five Fingers Play*

FIVE FINGERS PLAY

One finger points

Two fingers walk

Three fingers stand up and talk, talk, talk

Four fingers count 1, 2, 3, 4

Oh look, I've got one more! Five fingers, 1, 2, 3, 4, 5

Five fingers up

Five fingers down

Five fingers go round and round

Five fingers here

Five fingers there

Ten fingers to wash my hair

© 2003 Jan Z. Olsen

67

This finger–play is also found on the Sing Along CD #10. The activity uses movement and words to teach both body awareness and number skills.

Numbers, cont.

Teaching Wet-Dry-Try

The Wet–Dry–Try method is a sensory strategy to help children learn numbers without reversals. This teaching method works for all learning styles (visual, auditory, tactile, and kinesthetic) and is lots of fun

Gather Materials

Slate (1 per child)
Little chalk pieces
Little sponge pieces
Paper towel
Bowl of water

Teacher's Part

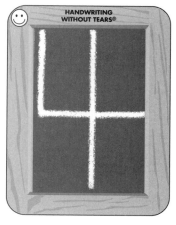

Demonstrate correct number formation.

Student's Part

WET
Wet tiny sponge. Squeeze out. With damp sponge, trace over the number like the teacher demonstrated. Wet index finger. Trace number again with your wet finger.

DRY
Use a small piece of paper towel to trace the number dry. Repeat two or three times.

TRY
Now, try writing the number with a small piece of chalk.

Tips for Teachers

- Use very little pieces of sponge and chalk—this helps develop the pencil grip.
- Squeeze the sponge well or the number will be too wet.
- This works best one–on–one or in centers with five or fewer students.
- To use this activity with the whole class you must pre–mark each student slate with the number (so they have a correct model to wet) and then demonstrate once for everyone.

Numbers, cont.

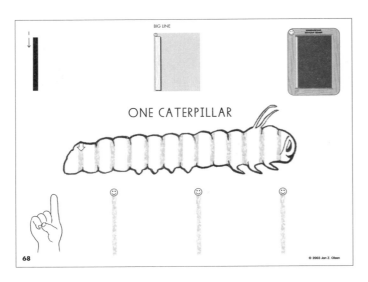

1 Caterpillar

Directions: Aim crayon at ☺. Big line down.
- Finger trace the number one at the top of the page.
- Teach one with wood pieces and on the slate.
- Count one caterpillar. Color the caterpillar.
- Make one with your finger. Trace the ones with a crayon.

1 with Bodies—Count on me! Animals too!
- Hold up one finger to show "one."
- Point with one finger.
- Count 1 on people. Count down the center.
  1 head, 1 forehead, 1 nose, 1 mouth, 1 chin,
  1 neck, 1 chest, 1 belly button.
- Count 1 on animal bodies! 1 head, 1 nose,
  l mouth, etc. Don't forget 1 tail!

1 with Objects—Count and compare
- Touch and count things one by one. Show children how to count in an organized way. Line up objects and count from left to right.
- Turn pages one by one.
- 1 on 1—At snack or mealtime, help children put 1 napkin on each mat, etc.
- 1 to 1—baby/crib, saddle/horse, hat/head, hot dog/ bun.
- Give just one when children ask for something. Then ask, "Do you want another one?

Number 1—See and say
- See "1" and say, "one."
- Look for numbers. Find "1."
- Say " first" and "first one." Talk about firsts—grade, day of school, birthday, snow of winter, star in the sky.
- Use "first" in a sequence. For example: First we put on our coats and then we go outside.
- Say who or what is first in a line. For example: A locomotive is the first car in the train.

2 Ducks

Directions: Aim crayon at ☺. Big curve. Little line.
- Finger trace the two at the top of the page.
- Teach two with wood pieces and on the slate.
- Count two ducks. Color the ducks.
- Hold up two fingers. Trace the twos with a crayon.

2 with Bodies—Count on me! Birds too!
- Hold up two fingers to show "2."
- Count 2 on our bodies! Count down the two sides! Use two pointer fingers. 2 eyebrows, 2 eyes, 2 ears, 2 cheeks 2 lips, etc.
- Count 2 on birds! Add verses for 2 wings and 2 eyes to the "Bird Legs" chant, track #12.

2 with Objects—Count and compare
- Count 2 on clothing! 2 shoes, 2 socks, 2mittens, 2 sleeves, 2 pant legs.
- Sort and match pairs by color and size.
- Share 2: 1 for me and 1 for you. Cut something in half to share.
- Count 2 wheels on bicycles. Compare with a tricycle.
- Put 2 candles on a cake, and count.

Numbers 2—See and say
- See "2" and say, "two."
- Look for numbers. Find "2."
- Say "second." Talk about second grade.
- Baseball? Show children first, second and third base. Run to second!
- Find numbers in Nursery Rhymes "One, two, button my shoe," etc.

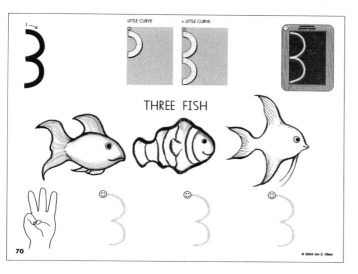

3 Fish

Directions: Aim crayon at ☺. Little curve. Little curve.
- Finger trace the three at the top of the page.
- Teach three with wood pieces and on the slate.
- Count three fish. Color the three fish.
- Hold up three fingers. Trace the threes with a crayon.

3 with Bodies—Count on me!
- Hold up three fingers to show "3."
- "3 fingers stand up and talk, talk, talk" (*Get Set for School™ Sing Along* CD #10)

3 with Objects—Count and compare
- Count 3 wheels on a tricycle.
- Touch and count 3 objects.
- Build a bridge with 2 cubes on bottom and one on top.
- Sort by category. Mix up 3 cars and 3 planes for child to divide into groups.
- Get ready with counting…1…2…3…go!
- Use 3 big lines to make a triangle. Count 3 sides and 3 angles.

Number 3—See and say
- See "3" and say, "three."
- Look for numbers. Find "3."
- Say "third." Do the children know a third grader?
- Baseball? Show children first, second and third base. Run to third!
- Find 3 in Nursery Rhymes "Old King Cole," "3 Blind Mice," "Rub a dub, dub, 3 men in a tub."

4 Animals

Directions: Aim crayon at ☺. Little line down. Little line across. Jump to the top. Big line down.
- Finger trace the four at the top of the page.
- Teach four with wood pieces and on the slate.
- Count four animals. Trace four legs.
- Hold up four fingers. Trace the fours with a crayon.

4 with Bodies—Count on me! Animals too!
- Hold up four fingers to show "4." How old are you?
- Creep on all 4s.
- "4 fingers count" when "Five Fingers Play." (*Get Set for School™ Sing Along* CD #10)
- Count 4 on animals. Add verses to the "Animal Legs" song, track #13, to include 4 legs on pet or wild animals (cats, dogs, zebras, elephants, etc.). Put the extra animals in a basket for this song.

4 with Objects—Count and compare
- Count 4 legs on chairs, 4 legs on tables and 4 wheels on cars!
- Touch and count 4 objects.
- Use 4 big lines to make a square
- Count 4 on a square napkin, 4 sides/4 corners. Open up the napkin and see 4 more squares.
- Count 4 birthday candles. How old are you?

Number 4—See and say
- See "4" and say, "four."
- Teach 4 year olds to say, "I am 4 years old."
- Look for numbers. Find "4."
- Say "fourth."
- Find 4 in Nursery Rhymes: "4 and 20 blackbirds baked in a pie."

Numbers, cont.

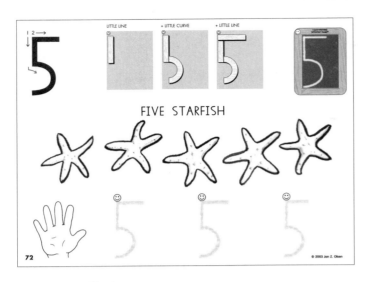

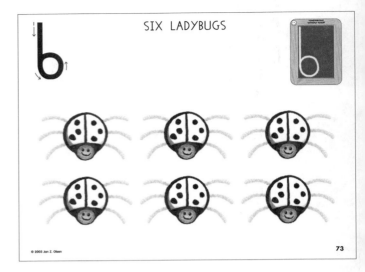

5 Starfish

Directions: Aim crayon at ☺. Little line down. Little curve. Jump to the ☺. Little line across.
- Finger trace the five at the top of the page.
- Teach five with wood pieces and on the slate.
- Count five starfish. Color five starfish.
- Hold up five fingers. Trace fives with a crayon.

5 with Bodies—Count on me! Animals too!
- Hold up your hand to show 5 fingers.
- Give me 5! Teach children how to give a high 5.
- Count toes on one foot. Now count the toes on the other foot!
- Sing the "Toe Song" on the Sing Along CD, track #11.
- Count 5 arms on a starfish.

5 with Objects—Count and compare
- Touch and count 5 objects.
- Count the points on a star.
- Count 5 birthday candles.

Number 5—See and say
- See "5" and say, "five."
- Teach 5 year olds to say, "I am 5 years old."
- Look for numbers. Find "5."
- Say "fifth."
- Play finger games with 5 "This is the beehive, Where are the bees?"
- Say the 5 days of the school week—Monday, Tuesday, Wednesday, Thursday, and Friday.

6 Ladybugs

- Finger trace the six at the top of the page.
- Count six ladybugs. Color six ladybugs.
- Trace six on the slate.

6 with Bodies—Count on me! Insects too!
- Hold up one hand for "5." Add one finger on the other hand for 6.
- Show children the hand motions for "The Ant, The Bug and The Bee" song, track #14.
  Hold up three fingers for "3."
  With two hands, that's "6 little legs."
  Walk them up and down in the air.
  Tuck hands in armpits when "they fly around."
  Continue with other motions.

6 with Objects—Count and compare
- Touch and count 6 objects.
- Build a tower with 6 cubes.
- Build a pyramid with 6 cubes, 3 on bottom, 2 in the middle, 1 on top.
- Put 6 eggs in an egg carton. Compare 6 eggs and 6 empty places.
- Use 12 eggs, 6 one color and 6 another color. Make color patterns.
- Make cardboard insects with egg cartons.

6 Numbers—To see and say
- See "6" and say, "six."
- Say "sixth."
- Look for numbers. Find "6." Look and count to 6 on a computer or calculator.
- Teach children to say dozen for 12 and half dozen for 6. Many children know these words from bagels or donuts.

Numbers, cont.

7 Turtles

- Finger trace the seven at the top of the page.
- Count seven turtles. Color seven turtles.
- Trace seven on the slate.

7 with Objects—Count and compare
- Touch and count 7 objects.
- Build a tower with 7 cubes.

7 Numbers—To see and say
- See "7" and say, "seven."
- Look for numbers. Find "7."
- Look and count to 7 on a computer or calculator.
- Say "seven days in the week."
- Fairy tale—"Snow White and the Seven Dwarfs."

8 Spiders

- Finger trace the eight at the top of the page.
- Count eight spiders. Color eight spiders.
- Trace eight on the slate.

8 with Bodies—Count on me! Spider and octopus too!
- Count legs on a spider. (Not a real one!)
- Show children the hand motions for "Spiders Love to Party," track #15.
  Hold up four fingers for "4."
  With two hands, that's "8 legs for dancing."
  Just dance around now. Feet really dance, but hands dance in air.
- Now have children sit down, lean back on their arms, and walk around on hands and feet, looking up. They'll be spiders dancing.
- Count legs on an octopus.

8 with Objects—Count and compare
- Touch and count 8 objects.
- Build a tower with 8 cubes.
- Count wheels on 2 cars.
- Craft—Make spiders by having children trace hands on folded black paper with white chalk. Teacher cuts this out and cuts off the "thumb." When opened, there's a spider.

Number 8—See and say
- See "8" and say, "eight."
- Count by twos: 2, 4, 6, 8.
- Look for numbers. Find "8."
- Find 8 on a clock. Is bedtime 8 o'clock? When does school start?

Numbers, cont.

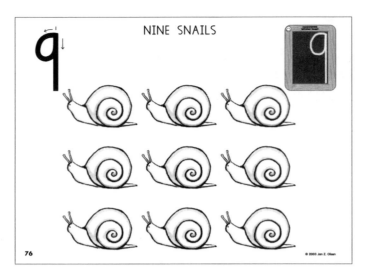

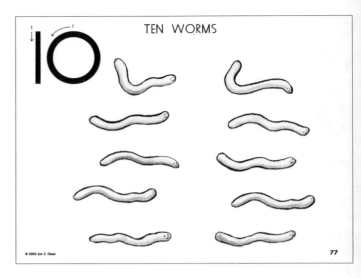

9 Snails

- Finger trace the nine at the top of the page.
- Count nine snails. Color nine snails.
- Trace nine on the slate.

9 with Objects—Count and compare
- Touch and count 9 objects.
- Build a tower with 9 cubes.

Number 9—See and say
- See "9" and say, "nine."
- Look for numbers. Find "9."
- Look and count to 9 on a computer or calculator.

10 Worms

- Finger trace the ten at the top of the page.
- Count ten worms. Color ten worms.

10 with Bodies—Count on me! Fingers and Toes!
- Hold up one hand for 5 and another hand for 5. That's 10 fingers!
- Use the "Five Fingers Play" chant on the Sing Along CD, track #10.
- Count toes on one foot. Now count the toes on the other foot!
- Sing the "Toe Song" on the Sing Along CD, track #11.

10 with Objects—To count and compare
- Touch and count 10 objects.
- Touch and count 10 pennies. Put 10 pennies in a bank.
- Look at a dime. It is equal to 10 pennies.

10 Numbers—To see and say
- See "10" and say, "ten."
- Look for numbers. Find "10."
- Look and count to 10 on a computer or calculator.
- Say "tenth."
- Count backward from 10.

Numbers, cont.

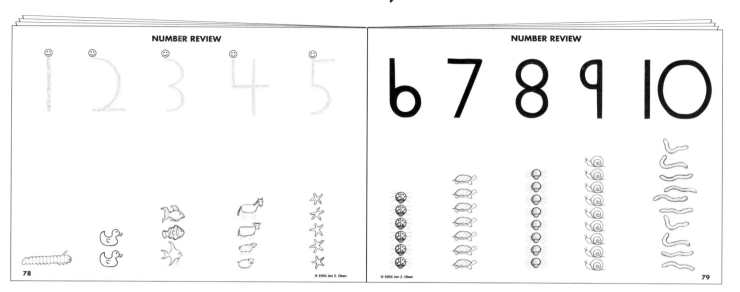

Teaching Number Review

Ask about numbers
Let's start with one and say the numbers. (In order)
If I point to a number, can you say the number? (Out of order)

Begin to look and learn
See the animals. They are in a line.
Compare the number of animals.
Teach or review the concept of "more."
Compare: Are there more: worms or caterpillars? fish or turtles?

Color and draw
Color the animals. They are so small!
Draw a line down from the number to the number of animals.

Demonstrate tracing 1 2 3 4 5
Let's trace the numbers.
Put the crayon on the ☺.
1 = Big line down
2 = Big curve—Little line across
3 = Little curve—Little curve
4 = Little line down—Little line across—Big line down
5 = Little line down—Little curve—Put the crayon on the ☺—Little line across

Extra
Show children how to line up objects for more accurate counting.
Help children touch and count small objects.
Use nursery rhymes and songs that use numbers.
Tap wood pieces. Have children listen and count the taps.
Use a Birthday Counting Verse such as:

Patrick has a birthday
We're so glad
We will see how many
He has had

As we count the candles
We are told (Count out loud as child places.)
Yes, the candles say,
He's 5 years old!

Alphabet—Writing Skills—Pages 85-86

Track #		
1	*Where Do You Start Your Letters?*	Point to the top
2	Alphabet Song	Sing ABC's
3	Alphabet Song (instrumental)	Sing ABC's
4	There's A Dog In The School	Bark and think the ABC's
5	Crayon Song	Prepare for holding crayon
6	*Magic C	Prepare for writing C and drawing circles
25	*Hokey Pokey	Learn words for making letters

Body Awareness and Number Skills—Page 87

7	Hello Song	Learn to shake hands with right hand
8	*Mat Man™	Build and draw a person, Numbers 1 + 2
9	Count On Me	Body math, Numbers 1, 2, 3, 4, 5, 6, 7, 8, 9, 10
10	Five Fingers Play	Fine motor finger–play, 1, 2, 3, 4, 5, 10
11	Toe Song	Body math, 5, 5, 10

Fine Motor Skills and Number Awareness—Page 88-89

8	*Mat Man™	1, 2—Count body parts
12	Bird Legs	2—Count one, two
13	Animal Legs	4—Count 2 in front, 2 in back, 4 legs in all, 1 tail
14	The Ant, The Bug, and The Bee	6—Finger–play, Make 3 + 3 with fingers, Imitate song motions
15	Spiders Love to Party	8—Dance, Make 4 + 4 with fingers
16	Ten Little Fingers	10—Fine motor finger–play

Drawing Skills—Page 90

6	*Magic C	Prepare for writing C and circles
8	*Mat Man™	Imitate teacher to draw a person
17	My Teacher Draws	Imitate teacher, Draw a circle, square and triangle

Listen, Move, and Imitate—Page 91-93

18	Puffy Fluffy	Move to music, Make clouds and rain in the air
19	Tap, Tap, Tap	Use two big lines to tap, follow rhythm and teacher's motions
20	Golden Slippers	Use two big lines to follow rhythm and teacher's motions
21	Skip to My Lou	Imitate teacher, Stop and start
22	Down on Grandpa's Farm	Imitate animal sounds
23	Peanut Butter and Jelly	Imitate movements
24	Rain Song	Imitate movements
25	*Hokey Pokey	Learn position words with wood pieces

* These songs appear in more than one category. They develop several skills.

CD Index

The first number is the CD track number. The bold numbers are Pre–K Teacher's Guide page references.

Track 1

Teacher's Guide,
p. 23

Tracks 2-3

Track 4

Alphabet—Writing Skills

Where Do You Start Your Letters?

Fun Focus: Point to the top, top, top.

Point to the top! That's where to start letters! This fun song teaches position concepts of top, middle, bottom while incorporating movement.

Alphabet Song/Instrumental

Fun Focus: Sing the ABC's with and without help.

It is fun to sing ABC's with others in a large group. Follow the children on the CD. They clearly sing every letter, even L M N O P!
A B C D E F G   H I J K   L M N O P   Q R S, T U V   W X, Y and Z
Now I know my A B Cs; Next time won't you sing with me.

Suggested Activities
- Sing while pointing to display cards in the classroom.
- Sing while pointing to page iv in the *Get Set for School*™ workbook.
- Try singing the ABC's with the instrumental version.

There's A Dog In the School

Fun Focus: Bark and think the ABC's.

Here's a chance to say the alphabet from a dog's point of view. This song will have your students barking the alphabet and laughing at the same time!

There's a dog in the school
Oh, no! What are we going to do?
As long as there are dogs in the school
They'll have to learn the alphabet too!

Ruff, ruff, ruff, ruff, ruff, ruff, ruff, etc.
Now I said my A B Cs, Next time won't you ruff with me!

Suggested Activities
- Sing (and bark) while pointing to ABC's on page iv of *Get Set for School*™ workbook.
- Sing (and bark) while teacher points to letter display cards.

Alphabet—Writing Skills, cont.

Crayon Song

Fun Focus: Children learn to pick up a crayon. Then they gently drop it and do it again. They love to drop.

Teaching proper grip has never been so easy or so much fun. Children enjoy learning that their fingers have important jobs! Getting to gently 'drop' crayons is an appealing surprise.

Pick up a crayon, Pick up a crayon, This is easy to do
Pick up a crayon, Pick up a crayon, I just tell my fingers what to do
My thumb is bent, Pointer points to the tip, Tall Man uses his side
I tuck my last two fingers in and take them for a ride

Now I'm holding it just right, But not too tight, Every finger knows what to do
And now I have a big surprise, A big surprise for you
Let's drop it and do it again!

Magic C

Fun Focus: Prepare for writing C and drawing circles.

Making C's and circles is easy when the teacher sings and shows children what to do. Children will remember which way to go.

Make a Magic C	Make a circle
I'll show you how	I'll show you how
Start at the top	Start with a C
Go this way now	Go this way now
Stop at the bottom	Keep on going
Look and see	Please don't stop
That Magic C looks good to me	It's a circle when you get to the top!
	Great job

Suggested Activities

- Teacher sings and demonstrates at the board or easel.
- Teacher holds up a big curve for C and points to the top of the C. The teacher sings and finger traces the C.
- For the next verse, start with a C and continue tracing to make a circle.
- Have children sing and finger trace big curves, C's and circles in their workbooks.

Body Awareness and Number Skills

Track 7
Teacher's Guide,
p. 15

Hello Song

Fun Focus: Learn to shake hands with right hand.

It's time to learn this important social skill. Children learn to look, to smile, and to shake hands with the right hand. Now it's easy to know which is the right hand.

Track 8
Teacher's Guide,
pp. 18–21

Mat Man™

Fun Focus: Build and draw a person. Learn 1 and 2. Count Mat Man's body parts.

This song helps children build Mat Man™ together as a group. Mat Man™ teaches body parts, body functions, and simple counting. After building Mat Man™, children learn to draw him too.

Track 9
Teacher's Guide,
p. 16

Count on Me

Fun Focus: Body math. Learn 1, 2, 1–10.

It's easy to help children count body parts. We are symmetrically made and our "two" body parts are on our two sides. The "one" body parts are down the center. Fingers and toes are in units of five.

Track 10
Teacher's Guide,
pp. 76, 79, 82

Five Fingers Play

Fun Focus: Fine motor finger–play, Learn 1, 2, 3, 4, 5 and 10.

Move those little fingers and learn numbers with this creative finger–play.

1 finger points	5 fingers up
2 fingers walk	5 fingers down
3 fingers stand up and talk, talk, talk	5.fingers go round and round
4 fingers count; 1, 2, 3, 4	5 fingers here
Oh look! I've got one more, 5 fingers	5 fingers there
	10 fingers to wash my hair

Suggested Activities

- Use as a finger–play. Follow the activity on page 76.
- Use to teach counting concepts.
- Preview adding concept of 5 and 5 makes 10 in all.

Track 11
Teacher's Guide,
pp. 17, 80, 82

Toe Song

Fun Focus: Body math, 5 + 5 make 10.

Children know and love the classic toe play, "This little piggy…"
This new song is fun too.

Fine Motor Skills and Number Awareness

Track 8
Teacher's Guide,
pp. 18–21

Mat Man™

Fun Focus: Count body parts.

Track 12
Teacher's Guide,
p. 50

Bird Legs

Fun Focus: 2 legs. Count 1 2.

No matter what they look like or what they do, birds have two!

2 4 6 8, We're counting legs so don't be late!

Quack, quack, peep, peep, Cock a doodle do
When we count the legs on birds
We always count 1 2

Red birds, black birds, pink birds too
When we count the legs on birds
We always count 1 2

Birds that fly, birds that float, birds that talk to you,
When we count the legs on birds
We always count 1 2

Birds that glide, birds that dive, birds that perch on yo
When we count the legs on birds
We always count 1 2

Suggested Activities

- Find pictures of birds and count the legs.
- Count wings or eyes on birds too.

Track 13
Teacher's Guide,
p. 79

Animal Legs

Fun Focus: 4 Legs! Count 2 in front, 2 in back, 4 legs in all, but just 1 tail!

Play the CD and then make up your own personalized versions with
new names and new animals. There are lots of four legged animals!

2 4 6 8, We're counting legs so don't be late!

We are counting legs
How many will there be?
Abi picks a **horse**
Let's look and see
2 legs in the front, 2 legs in the back
The horse has 4 legs
I know that! But only 1 tail
Neighhhhh

We are counting legs
How many will there be?
Meagan picks a **lamb**
Let's look and see
2 legs in the front, 2 legs in the back
The lamb has 4 legs
I know that! But only 1 tail
Baaaa

We are counting legs
How many will there be?
Charlie picks a **cow**
Let's look and see
2 legs in the front, 2 legs in the back
The cow has 4 legs
I know that! But only 1 tail
Mooooo

We are counting legs
How many will there be?
Patrick picks a **pig**
Let's look and see
2 legs in the front, 2 legs in the back
The pig has 4 legs
I know that! But only 1 tail
Ooink, ooink, And it's a curly little tail!

Suggested Activities

- Change the names and animals. Count the legs and tails on the animals.
- Change the song to "We are counting wheels, How many
  will there be?" Use cars, trucks, bicycles and tricycles.

Fine Motor Skills and Number Awareness, cont.

Track 14

Teacher's Guide,
pp. 43, 55, 80

The Ant, The Bug, and The Bee

Fun Focus: Learn 6 with insect legs.

Suggested Activities

- Use this song as a finger–play. Children can use three fingers on each hand and pretend that their finger are insect legs. They can move their hands up and down and then tuck them in for wings.
- Color ants, bugs, and bees in the workbook pages 4 and 5.

Track 15

Teacher's Guide,
p. 81

Spiders Love to Party

Fun Focus: Learn 8 with spider legs.

It's fun to sing and dance around the room and think of spiders having 8 legs.

Spiders love to party
They love to celebrate
And when those spiders party
They shimmy and they shake

**Chorus
With 8 legs for dancing
They sure can cut a rug
With 8 legs for dancing
They do the jitterbug**

Some spiders do the tango
And some do "do–si–do"
And some just take those 8 legs
And kick 'em to and fro
Chorus

So if you see a spider
Just take a second glance
See if that old spider
Is going to a dance

Chorus

And when the dancing's over
It's time to go to bed
They waltz home on 8 legs
And tuck them in a web

**Chorus
(Repeat 1X)**

That's right...yeah!

Suggested Activities

- Use this song as a finger–play. Children tuck in their thumbs and dance around with "eight legs."
- Use this song as a gross motor activity and crawl around on the floor like large spiders.

Track 16

Teacher's Guide,
p. 35

Ten Little Fingers

Fun Focus: Fine motor finger–play.

Finger–plays are perfect for developing fine motor and imitating skills.
This will be a favorite.

Drawing Skills

Track 6
Teacher's Guide,
pp. 57–58

Track 8
Teacher's Guide,
pp. 18–21

Track 17
Teacher's Guide,
pp. 34, 51, 52,
54, 60, 69,
75

Magic C

Fun Focus: Prepare for writing C and drawing circles.

Mat Man™

Fun Focus: Imitate the teacher to draw a person.

My Teacher Draws

Fun Focus: Imitate teacher. Draw a circle, square, and triangle.

Children love to have grown ups draw for them. Watching the
teacher draw prepares children for drawing today or another day.

My teacher draws
Some shapes for me
What's this shape?
Let's look and see
It's a circle
The circle gets eyes, nose, mouth, pointy ears, and whiskers too
Now what can this circle do?
It can be a kitty cat!

My teacher draws
Some shapes for me
What's this shape?
Let's look and see
It's a square
The square gets windowpanes, windowsill, and curtains too!
Now what can this square do?
It can be a window!

My teacher draws
Some shapes for me
What's this shape?
Let's look and see
It's a triangle
The triangle gets squirting fire, rocks, and lava too!
Now what can this triangle do?
It can be a volcano!

Suggested Activities

- While teaching shapes on pages 20, 22, 26, 36, 54, 55, and 66 in the *Get Set for
  School*™ workbook, use this song. As you sing the lyrics draw extra parts to turn the
  shape into a fun drawing. This helps children with pre–drawing skills.
- Use paper plates and cut outs to make kitty cats.

90

Listen, Move, and Imitate

Track 18
Teacher's Guide,
p. 49

Track 19
Teacher's Guide,
p. 14

Track 20

Track 21

Puffy Fluffy

Fun Focus: Move to music, Make clouds and rain in the air.

Tap, Tap, Tap

Fun Focus: Use two big lines to tap, follow the rhythm and the teacher's motions.

Golden Slippers (instrumental)

Fun Focus: Use two big lines to follow rhythm and teacher's motions.

This upbeat instrumental was added for extra practice tapping.
Children can imitate the teacher's movements and tapping patterns.
Change movement when the music changes.

Skip to My Lou

Fun Focus: Imitate teacher. Stop and start.

It's fun to move to the music when the verses change. Just follow the teacher!

Lost my partner what'll I do? Repeat 2X
Skip to my Lou my darling...
Skip, skip, skip to my Lou, Repeat 2X
Skip to my Lou my darling...FREEZE

Flies in the buttermilk shoo fly shoo,
Repeat 2X
Hop to my Lou my darling
Hop, hop, hop to my Lou, Repeat 2X
Hop to my Lou my darling...FREEZE

You swing me and I'll swing you, Repeat 2X
Tip toe my Lou my darling
Tip toe, tip toe, My Lou, Repeat 2X
Tip toe, My Lou my darling....FREEZE

Lost my partner what'll I do? Repeat 2X
March to my Lou my darling

March, march, march to my Lou, Repeat 2X
March to my Lou my darling...FREEZE

Flies in the buttermilk shoo fly shoo, Repeat
2X
Gallop to my Lou my darling
Gallop, gallop to my Lou, Repeat 2X
Gallop to my Lou my darling...FREEZE

You swing me and I'll swing you, Repeat 2X
Tip toe my Lou my darling
Tip toe, tip toe my Lou, Repeat 2X
Tip toe, My Lou my darling....FREEZE

You swing me and I'll swing you, Repeat 2X
Tip toe my Lou my darling
Jump, jump, jump to my Lou, Repeat 2X
Jump to my Lou my darling.....FREEZE

Suggested Activities
- Use this song as a gross motor activity.
  Each verse has a different gross motor movement.
- Use this song to teach the concept of start/stop.
  The music freezes between verses.

Listen, Move, and Imitate, cont.

Down on Grandpa's Farm

Fun Focus: Sing and imitate animal sounds.

The surprise is a banjo. When children learn letter sounds, it's very helpful to think of animals having a name and making a sound. Letters do the same.

Oh down on Grandpa's farm there is a **big brown cow**
Down on Grandpa's farm there is a big brown cow
The cow, it goes a lot like this (moo)
The cow, it goes a lot like this (moo)
We're on our way, we're on our way, On our way to Grandpa's farm Repeat 1X

Oh down on Grandpa's farm there is a **little white chicken** Repeat 1X
The chicken, it goes a lot like this (cluck, cluck) Repeat 1X
We're on our way, we're on our way, On our way to Grandpa's farm Repeat 1X

Oh down on Grandpa's farm there is a **little spotted goat** Repeat 1X
The goat, it goes a lot like this (naaah, naaah) Repeat 1X
We're on our way, we're on our way, On our way to Grandpa's farm Repeat 1X

Oh down on Grandpa's farm there is an **old banjo**. Repeat 1X
The banjo, it goes a lot like this (plucka, plucka, plucka) Repeat 1X
We're on our way, we're on our way, On our way to Grandpa's farm Repeat 3X

Suggested Activities
- Sing before taking a field trip to a farm or while learning about farms and animals.
- Add new verses naming things and sounds you see and hear on a farm.

Listen, Move, and Imitate, cont.

Track 23

Peanut Butter and Jelly

Fun Focus: Imitate movements.

We added this one because the tune, the words, and the motions are so much fun!

Chorus
Peanut, peanut butter ....**And jelly**
Peanut, peanut butter ....**And jelly**

Now first you take the peanuts and you grind them, you grind them   Repeat 1X, **Chorus**
Put one fist on top of the other and grind back and forth.

And then you take the grapes and you squish them, and you squish them   Repeat 1X, **Chorus**
Squish pretend grapes between your fingers.

And then you take the bread and you spread, and you spread   Repeat 1X, **Chorus**
Hold one hand out flat like bread and spread with the other hand.

And then you take the pieces and you put them together   Repeat 1X, **Chorus**
Clap your hands together.

And then you take your lunch and you munch, and you munch   Repeat 1X, **Chorus**
Take a big bite out of the sandwich!

Mm,mm,mm,mm,mm,mm,mm,mm,mm   Repeat 1X, **Chorus 2X**
Rub your tummy in a circle.

Suggested Activities
- Encourage a variety of movements, listening and following directions.

*Traditional, arrangement by Cathy Fink, © 2 Spoons Music, ASCAP Licensed from the recording "Grandma Slid Down the Mountain" on Rounder Records

Track 24
Teacher's Guide,
p. 56

Rain Song

Fun Focus: Imitate falling rain motions. Color page 30 in the workbook.

Most children have boots and love to kick or play in puddles.

Track 25
Teacher's Guide,
p. 9

Hokey Pokey

Fun Focus: Move wood pieces up, down and all around.

Check Readiness

This is your guide to the informal readiness check found in the student workbook, *Get Set For School*™ on pages 80 and 81. Please copy those pages and use them to check readiness skills.

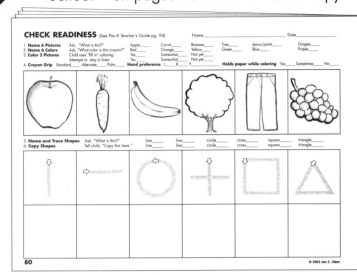

General Directions: Check each correct item. Write in other answers and observations.

1. Name 6 Pictures Typically, this is easy for English speaking children. When asking a non-verbal child to point, name the pictures in random order.

2. Name 6 Colors Use crayons with true colors. Ask the child to say the colors as you point.

3. Color 2 Pictures Let the child choose the pictures to color. Notice how the child picks up and uses crayons. Record this on the next item.

4. Crayon Grip
Hand Preference
Holds Paper
See pages 32–38 for information about these skills.
Note which hand is used. Mark a "?" if the child changes hands when coloring.

5. Name and Trace Shapes Children may use other words, for example: one for line, or ball for circle. Simply write the child's words on the page. Tell the child to start on the arrow and trace the shapes.

6. Copy Shapes As soon as the child finishes each shape, make a dot to show the starting place. This will make you aware of the child's starting tendency.

7. Draw a Person Name, date and save these. Check the 10 parts and note any "extras."

8. Name 10 Letters Naming letters out of order shows true recognition. Write in any wrong answers. When asking a non-verbal child to point, say the letters in random order.

9. Name 9 Numbers Write in any wrong answers. When asking a non-verbal child to point, say the numbers in random order.

10. Try to Write Name Tell child to start at the ☺. As soon as the child writes a letter, make a dot to show the starting place.

Help Me Hold the Crayon

There are easy ways to help your child. Even if you're not a teacher, and don't hold the pencil correctly yourself, you can still be a very good influence on your child. Here's how:

1. Choose the right writing tools.
2. Show your child how to hold them.
3. Be a good example.

How do I choose the right writing tools?

- As soon as your child is past age 3 or the "puts things in his mouth, swallowing" stage, give your child little broken pieces of chalk or crayon to use and lots of big sheets of paper for free scribbling/drawing.
- Little pieces of finger food also encourage finger skills.

Why little pieces?

Little pieces develop fingertip control and strength. They encourage the precise pinch that's used for crayons and pencils. Notice how well your child uses his/her fingers with little pieces. There's research to show that starting with small pieces encourages the correct grasp.

What about regular crayons and pencils?

They're fine, but you must show your child how to hold and use them. Save the pencils for later. Pencils are sharp pointed sticks and really aren't appropriate for beginners. Fat pencils and crayons are too heavy for little hands.

When should I start?

Right now. You can start showing your child how to use crayons as soon as your child wants to color.

How do I show my child?

1. Teach your child to name the first 3 fingers – the thumb, the "pointer", and the "tall man."
2. Move them - Give a "thumbs up" and wiggle the thumb. Have your child point with the pointer finger and then put the "tall man" beside the pointer finger.
3. Make a big open "O" pinch – this positions the thumb and pointer correctly.

What is the correct grip?

Here's a picture. Notice that there is a choice. Some children like to "pinch" with the thumb and pointer. That's the tripod (3—pinch with thumb and pointer, pencil rests on tall man). Others like the quadropod (4–pinch with thumb and pointer/tall man together, pencil rests on ring finger).

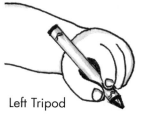
Left Tripod
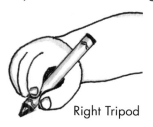
Right Tripod
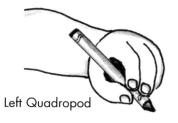
Left Quadropod

Right Quadropod

What else can I do?

1. Pick up and Drop it! This is a fun way to practice placing the fingers correctly. Help your child pick up the pencil and get all the fingers placed. Then drop it! See if your child can put all the fingers back in the right place again. Repeat two or three times.
2. Aim and Scribble. Make tiny stars or spots on paper. Teach your child how to aim the crayon and land on a star to make it shine. Help the crayon hand rest on the paper, with the elbow down and the hand touching the paper. Help the helper hand hold the paper. Now just wiggle the fingers to scribble.
3. Show your child how to hold and move the crayon to make different strokes, back and forth, up and down, round and round.

Help Me Write My Name

"That's my name. My name starts with _____." Maybe your child is trying to write or even make letters you can recognize. If so, then it's time to start showing your child how to write a few letters. Here's how:

1. Be a good example.
2. Write in all capital letters.
3. Start every letter at the top.
4. Teach letters step by step.
5. Write on paper strips with a ☺ in the top left corner.

How can I be a good example?
Hold the crayon correctly. Your child will be watching both how you make the letters and how you hold the pencil. Be sure to be a good model. Make a special effort to hold the crayon (or pencil) correctly when you write for your child.

Why should I use all capitals?
Capitals are the first letters to learn. Capitals are the first letters children can visually recognize and remember. Capitals are the first letters children can physically write.

Does it matter where my child starts letters?
It really does. English has one basic rule for both reading and writing: read and write English from top to bottom, left to right. When you write with your child, always start at the top. Write letters top to bottom and left to right.

What do I say when I teach the letters?
This is easy. Always say, "I start at the top." Then describe the part you're making. Say "big" or "little" for size. Say "line" or "curve" for shape, like this: D = "I make a big line. Now I make a big curve." See the ABC chart to check the words.

What kind of paper should I use?
Just fold a paper in half the long way and then in half again. Cut. That will give you four strips, about 2" by 11". You can adjust the size if your child needs to write bigger. Now put a ☺ in the top left corner of each strip. Use two strips. You write on the top one; your child writes on the bottom one. Make the capital letters as big as the paper.

What about hard letters?
Some letters, like S or diagonal letters like M and N are tricky. You can write with a highlighter pen on your child's paper to help guide your child.

What about lowercase letters?
Lowercase letters are for children in kindergarten. Wait until your child is at the kindergarten level and knows the capitals before you introduce lowercase letters. The skills your child learns with capitals will help your child succeed with lowercase letters.

Help Me Write My Name, cont.

Using CAPITAL STRIPS

Since we teach developmentally, we write "NAME" in Pre-K and transition to "Name" in kindergarden.

Why CAPITALS first?
- Capitals are the easiest letters to write.
- Capitals are easy to recognize and are familiar.
- Capitals are the same height.
- Capitals start at the same place, the top.
- Capitals are in the same position.

Use CAPITAL STRIPS with a ☺ for instruction. Put your strip above the child's strip. Demonstrate each letter on your strip and wait for the child to imitate you. Do this letter by letter. (See below.) If the child needs a model to trace, use a highlighter. Don't use dots. They make it difficult for the child to see the letter as a whole symbol.

Tips for Parents
- Don't worry about using lowercase letters. Children will transition to using a beginning capital and lowercase in kindergarten. Lowercase letters are too difficult for preschoolers.
- Be sure that the children start every letter at the top. See the attached letter chart for letter formation.
- You can vary the size of the CAPITAL STRIPS to suit the child's size preference. Remember to put a ☺ in the top left corner as a cue for right side up and where to start.
- If a child has already been taught to use lowercase, that's fine too. Just check to see if the letters are formed correctly. Remember that no letters ever start at the bottom. Not even lowercase letters.

Parent or Teacher strip

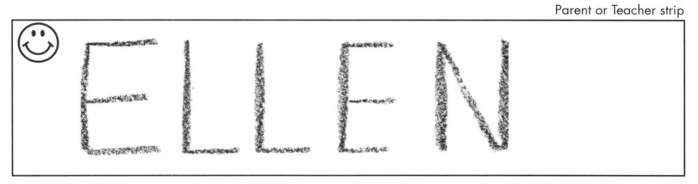

Child strip

© 2005 Jan Z. Olsen

Dear Parents,

We are excited about the Pre-K curriculum we are using. It has won the Distinguished Achievement Award for the best children's curriculum as well as a Teacher's Choice Award from *Learning Magazine*. This Pre–K curriculum develops coloring, drawing, counting, and handwriting readiness. The program uses music, multi-sensory learning materials and the "crayon only" *Get Set for School* workbook.

During the year, we will introduce new activities. The children will build Mat Man™ on the floor with wood pieces and draw a picture of him. They'll make capital letters and numbers with wood pieces and dough. Music is important! Just wait… you will soon be hearing new songs for letters, counting and even for fingers and toes!

We will be teaching important pre-writing and alphabet skills. We are sending home information so that you'll know what we're teaching and how to help at home. Please let us know if you have any questions.

Sincerely,

P.S. If you would like more information about the Get Set for School program visit the Handwriting Without Tears® website; www.hwtears.com.

Learning Magazine
2005 Winner
Teacher's Choice Award

Association for
Educational Publishers
2005 Winner
Children's Curriculum

Get Set for School™
Sing Along CD

Recorded by 2004 and 2005 Grammy
winning artists, Cathy & Marcy

98

A
Big line
Big line
Little line

B
Big line
Little curve
Little curve

C
Big C curve

D
Big line
Big curve

E
Big line
Little line
Little line
Little line

F
Big line
Little line
Little line

G
Big curve
Little line
Little line

H
Big line
Big line
Little line

I
Big line
Little line
Little line

J
Big line
Turn
Little line

K
Big line
Little line
Little line

L
Big line
Little line

M
Big line
Big line
Big line
Big line

N
Big line
Big line
Big line

O
Big C curve
Keep going

P
Big line
Little curve

Q
Big C curve
Keep going
Little line

R
Big line
Little curve
Little line

S
Little curve
Turn
Little curve

T
Big line
Little line

U
Big line
Turn
Big line

V
Big line
Big line

W
Big line
Big line
Big line
Big line

X
Big line
Big line

Y
Little line
Big line

Z
Little line
Big line
Little line